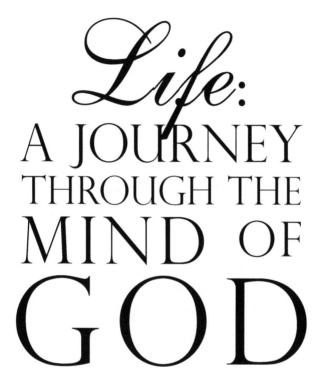

Life:
A JOURNEY
THROUGH THE
MIND OF
GOD

EARL D. RAGLAND

authorHOUSE®

AuthorHouse™
1663 Liberty Drive
Bloomington, IN 47403
www.authorhouse.com
Phone: 1 (800) 839-8640

Published by AuthorHouse 11/27/2017

ISBN: 978-1-5462-1825-8 (sc)
ISBN: 978-1-5462-1826-5 (e)

Print information available on the last page.

For in him we live and move and
have our being. -Acts 17:28

Contents

Introduction

Life has been called a "journey." Indeed, it is named aptly so, for as in a journey, the course of living is not stationary, but an ever-moving procession of events and experiences.

From generation to generation human beings have proceeded along their collective and individual paths developing belief systems; concepts and values that shape their overall perceptions of life and reality. To many, life is a fathomless enigma filled with boundless possibilities.

Thus, belief systems, concepts and values are developed in a countless variety of ways. These differing views are as expansive as the range of human imagination.

But man's "journey"; or his pursuit of life was designed by his Maker to ultimately be one of eternal fellowship with his own glorified children. God is involved in man's purpose, for it is He who has *given* man purpose. And God had a definite and eternal purpose for creating man and making this planet earth his home. So then, while filled with countless mysteries, life is clearly ***more*** than mere chance or possibility.

But undeniably, the elements of chance and possibility loom large in our lives. Yet, there is the existence of **certainty**; even if the fact is that only God has the absolute sense of it. Certainty for us is defined as strong belief that what we conceive and accept in our minds to be true is in fact, true. Certainty is strong conviction, and that is as far as we can humanly take the matter. A man can search for what could be; determine what can be, but only God knows in every case with certainty, what is. We fallible humans have a limited degree of "*certainty*" *available to us. I have been certain about a few things over the years that have proven to be inaccurate. I must inquire: have you?*

The things that we believe with all our hearts are the things that we dare to boldly declare that we know! And things that we have come to fully and deeply believe, establish our identity and shape our character. A child for example; that was raised in a negativity-filled environment and told repeatedly that it was dumb or ugly will usually eventually be convinced that it is true, although the truth may be that the child is neither dumb nor ugly. But because of this, many negative attitudes and hurtful behaviors have been provided an avenue for development in such children and usually do. Adults for example, who suffered abuse as children, have many times developed sadistic personality traits. It is a true saying that: "Hurt people hurt people." These people project their own inner suffering onto others.

Conversely, in a positive environment where children are encouraged, and time is taken with them, they are made to feel valuable and confidence is instilled in them. These are more likely to thrive.

But in either case, neither success nor failure are certain or automatic. For example, those who were voted "most likely to succeed" in high school have in some cases, lived out their days in abject failure, while some others that nearly everyone had 'written off" and labeled "loser" have defied the odds; contradicted the naysayers and lived highly successful and productive lives. **In a world of time, chance and choice-driven destiny, nothing is guaranteed but the eternal purpose of God.**

*<u>There are many beliefs; but truth is another matter altogether</u>; especially, eternal truth. There are **natural truths** in this material world that have been searched out, discovered and understood through human intellect & reason. But there are also **spiritual truths** that must be "spiritually discerned". I speak here, of two very different processes, but God is the Source of all truth. Indeed, truth is a fundamental quality of his unchangeable nature.*

Eternal truth is revealed to some, and concealed from others.

God reveals *divine truth* to those who have been "spiritually awakened", and have a heart's desire to know Him and learn of his ways. Jesus said that those who desired to do the will of God will know of his teaching. (John 7:17). The grand truth is that life in all its reality is according to God's eternal purpose.

Human understanding of many things is often faulty, and many times these errors are expanded, propagated and perpetuated from one generation to another.

Actually, there are many things that contribute to the development of our interpretations of reality. But the life-laws of time and chance do not always flow in sync with the belief systems that we have grown into, thus life does not always co-operate with our hopes, expectations or convictions.

This book is about the spiritual truths that undergird the natural truths of this consciousness we call "life".

The grand truth expressed in this book is that life in all its reality is according to God's purpose.

I claim no exclusive revelation. Whatever I have learned, others have learned in greater abundance long before me. It is also doubtless to me that there are a host of others who could elucidate the very truths that I will share with far greater clarity and eloquence. But I am what I am, and offer what I have to give with the degree of capability with which I have been blessed.

I pray that this spiritual offering will be a blessing to all who read and consider the things I share; some prayerfully, and some who will not necessarily pray but will yet have an open and receptive mind.

Sincerely in the service of God,

Earl D. Ragland

CHAPTER 1

What is Life?

Let's say you are a middle-aged father with an 18-year-old son or daughter who come to you and say they need to have a talk with you.

It is clear to you that your child is serious, so you set aside whatever you had been thinking about and give your undivided attention.

The conversation goes something like this: "You know dad, life is very confusing to me right now." "Lately, I've been wrestling with so many questions." "It is not the first time these sorts of questions have arisen in my mind, but the other times, I just said to myself, I don't know, and just dismissed them. I guess I figured, that's just the way things are." But the older I get; the more I think about the things I hear and see; the things I feel." "Now, when I look out at the world around me, I have this sensation of feeling overwhelmed with questions for which I have no answers."

1

"It just seems that life is filled with such possibility, yet such uncertainty." "Dad, what is life?"

Whoa! You didn't see that coming, did you?

Yet you know that this is no time for a pat answer or a cliché' because it occurs to you that he or she has already heard every one of them that you ever knew.

Whatever your perception of life and reality was, in the rearing of your children, you have passed it on to them both by precept and example.

Perhaps you have taught them to believe in God and that life happens according to his will.

Perhaps you told them that God is love, just like the scriptures say.

Let's just examine these two pieces of information for a few minutes, and let's place them in this scenario: The two of you are sitting in the living room and the TV is on with the volume turned down, but the two of you are still able to see and hear it in the background while you talk.

You said, "Life happens according to God's will." Then, you said, "God is love."

At the completion of that statement, the two of you are distracted by a popular news anchor with a ("This Just In"); or ("Breaking news). "American troops suffer casualties because of the escalation of intense ground fighting in the region." "Administration seems to be at a quandary regarding ongoing strategy as the nation finds itself embroiled in three separate international conflicts." "Meanwhile, the domestic economic outlook for the coming months seems to provide no assurance of an upturn."

You have both looked away from one another to see and hear the report that drew your attention.

When the report is over, you look back at each other, and without a word, it is clear before resuming the conversation, that the report itself has provided a case in point.

If life happens according to the will of God, and God is love, why all the fighting and killing and poverty and hatred and racism, and sexual abuse, and on, and on, and on? This is the will of a loving God?

Perhaps these are questions that you yourself have been unwilling to seriously ask for fear of what might be revealed to you. Perhaps through the sincere search for meaning being shared with you by your offspring, for the first time in your own life, you find yourself confronted with questions that challenge your long-held beliefs.

This little scenario was presented to raise the question: Indeed; What Is life?

That question has certainly been widely and continually asked by people of every generation since the earliest years of human history.

And since after so many centuries the question is still being asked today, it is clear that for most, it continues to be an unsolved mystery.

Many have overtly examined countless theories in pursuit of answers, but all of us have, to some extent, been unconsciously and passively programmed by our experiences. A set of beliefs has been developed in us all. And there is an endless range of diversity among us in defining the answer to that question.

Yet as humans, we share our thoughts; our values and convictions, indeed, our lives with one another, however we may define them. In doing so, we establish relationships. We can establish relationships because of the universal commonality of human nature.

From the beginning of human history, we have been able to observe one another and recognize common qualities and appealing differences. Endowed with the natural ability to relate and communicate, we are attracted to one another. Thus, we pursue relationships. There is obviously, an endless variety of ways that people relate to one another and many of these relationships continue to become unions which reproduce new generations.

So then, the concept of ***relationships*** is simply and clearly an undeniable foundation stone in the structure of life.

But any of us may either share, or generally conceal and privately maintain our personal thoughts, feelings, desires and choices; for we are also aware of our own ***individuality.***

It cannot be denied that there is a sense in which we are indeed individual selves. We may be able to relate to each other, but I am not you, and you are not me.

We may through relationships, know **who** we are, but these relationships do not clearly reveal to us, **what** we are; and even more perplexing: **why** we are!

Again, we all have a way of seeing life; a *worldview,* or what we perceive to be real. What is life to you? How do you see the world; and more specifically, your place in it? Can it be denied that we all have certain preconceptions that influence our view of life?

Are your views of life and reality founded upon deeply held convictions, or have they been more casually conceived, resulting from the act of avoiding any thoughtful or in-depth considerations of the subject?

All of us are unavoidably influenced by so many things; one's culture, home environment, individual experiences, genetic predisposition, etc.;

But even as we are conscious of our own existence and the world around us, should we simply live out our days until we pass on, never seriously entertaining the question of our reason for being?

There are many <u>theories</u>, but <u>what</u> <u>is</u> <u>the</u> <u>truth</u>?

Collectively; generically, we call ourselves "man"; or mankind, but what is our reason for being; our real significance? From whence have we come and to what or Whom shall we arrive?

The worldview that is the inspiration of this book is theological, but *specifically* biblical. So then, let us examine this question of life by way of the sacred scriptures.

In **the book of Psalms**, David, the great ancient king of Israel expressed his desire to understand these things.

In **144 3**, He considers the infinite greatness of God and the apparent insignificance of man: **"LORD, what is man, that you take knowledge of him; or the son of man, that you make account of him!"**

In essence, David is saying to God: "LORD, what really are we human creatures; and why do we matter to you?" David continues in **verse 4: "Man is like to vanity: his days are as a shadow that passes away."** In other words, unless there is more to man than what can be observed outwardly, this brief tenure we call "life" is seemingly, a mere pointless journey back to the dust from which we originated. If this is so, then no sense can be made of life.

The book of Ecclesiastes is also filled with observations about our natural lives in the world. The entire book is an examination of life "under the sun"; in other words, a study of life in this visible, material world.

The book is filled with wise insights to help one discover the "temporarily meaningful" features of this short-term residency on earth; a way of living in order to experience the good of life until death arrives to usher man back to the dust.

Observe now, the words of **Solomon,** the son and successor of King David, who continues the theme of his father concerning the vanity of this present life and how we should make the best of the time we are granted. (in 9 2 thru 13 – God's Word Version):

(2) "Everything turns out the same way for everyone. (That is; in the end, we all die. - (My added comment)

"All people will share the same destiny, (in other words; eventually die) whether they are righteous, wicked, or good, clean or unclean, whether they offer sacrifices or don't offer sacrifices." "Good people are treated like sinners. People who take oaths are treated like those who are afraid to take oaths.

(3) This is the tragedy of everything that happens under the sun: Everyone shares the same destiny. Moreover, the hearts of mortals are full of evil. (In other words; since all people are destined to die, they give themselves over to every sort of evil because to them, it doesn't matter. (My added comments)

Madness is in their hearts while they are still alive. After that, they join the dead. (4) But all who are among the living have hope, because a living dog is better than a dead lion.

(5) The living know that they will die, but the dead don't know anything. (In other words; The living is still able to think and act before they die, but the dead are incapable of

doing anything else in this world. - (My comments added) There is no more reward for the dead when the memory of them has faded.

(6) Their love, their hate, and their passions have already vanished. They will never again take part in anything that happens under the sun.

(7) Go, enjoy eating your food, and drink your wine cheerfully, because God has already accepted what you've done. (8) Always wear clean clothes, and never go without lotion on your head. (9) Enjoy life with your wife, whom you love, during all your brief, pointless life. God has given you your pointless life under the sun. This is your lot [in life] and what you get for the arduous work that you do under the sun.

(10) Whatever presents itself for you to do, do it with [all] your might, because there is no work, planning, knowledge, or skill in the grave where you're going.

(11) I saw something else under the sun. The race isn't [won] by fast runners, or the battle by heroes. Wise people don't necessarily have food. Intelligent people don't necessarily have riches, and skilled people don't necessarily receive special treatment. But time and unpredictable events overtake all of them.

(12) No one knows when his time will come. Like fish that are caught in a cruel net or birds caught in a snare, humans are trapped by a disaster when it suddenly strikes them.

(13) I also have seen this example of wisdom under the sun, and it made a deep impression on me."

I believe that if there is one matter that concerns us all and "magnetically" draws our attention towards a deeper consideration of life, it is the matter of death. The natural aging process makes us aware of the dissipation of our life force. And because of the seemingly random and indiscriminate nature of death, not even the young enjoy full immunity from considerations of their own mortality. Every funeral attended; every eulogy heard tends to cause us, if only for a short season, to think more seriously about the significance of our earthly pilgrimage.

Here is what King Solomon says: "The heart of the wise is in the house of mourning; but the heart of fools is in the house of mirth."(Ecclesiastes 7 4)

Let's read a few more of these verses in the God's Word Version: (2) It is better to go to a funeral than to a banquet because that is where everyone will end up. Everyone who is alive should take this to heart! (3) Sorrow is better than laughter because, despite a sad face, the heart can be joyful. (4) The minds of wise people think about funerals, but the minds of fools think about banquets.

We all realize that none of us can naturally know with certainty when death will arrive for us. So then, when that time comes; when I am no longer able to participate in the events occurring on this earth; not with my family, friends, neighbors, co-workers; when I have no part, nor lot in the things done here, what will my journey have meant? To whom will it have mattered? Somehow, to King David's amazement; and to my own, when it will not matter to anyone else on this whole earth, ...it will matter to God!

For the majority of us ordinary folk who will depart from this world never becoming famous, within fifty years of our departure, practically no one will ever know we were ever here. For some of us, this will be true much sooner. When we consider life from this perspective and think about the verses we have just read, the context in which both King David and King Solomon speak of "vanity" is clear to us.

To this very day, a key element of the values of all men and women of this world is established on the principle of human mortality. We were born; we live, and we will die. This is an obvious truth.

But it is this brief living space that intrigues us. Undoubtedly, within each of us, as it was with King Solomon, so with us, this question of life generates a broad range of thoughts, feelings, imaginations and memories that somehow articulate the nature of our experience. This mystery-filled, imagination-stimulating question opens to both thoughtful and shallow minds, the door to an endless array of differing opinions and worldviews.

So then, if we are being asked to describe how we perceive our conscious experience in the world, within many of us, there is an on-demand "Life to me is this", response.

Ok then, so here's another question. If each of us has a 'host' of individualized theories and personal concepts, who then, has the **authoritative** description; the **official definition**, if you will, of this illusive, intriguing little four-letter word? Is there a singular, "one-size-fits-all" model we all can use as a sort of "philosophical template"? The simple answer to this question is **"yes" there is.**

To many, it appears that the only guarantee about life is that there are no guarantees. To many, life just is.

*But the truth is that **life is the conception of an omniscient God** who is what he is, and will be what he will be. **It is He who has given life its meaning and purpose.** And the divine guarantee is that God's ultimate will, and purpose will abide for all eternity.*

As for finite unbelieving man, he will continue to search for life's meaning as well as deeper insights in the quest to define his own self until he comes to the realization that without God's inspiration, he is engaged in a futile exercise.

When sin-bound, sense-ruled men have examined all the conflicting ideas and opinions that they can bear; when the many theories and speculations that intrigued them have been so intermingled with unanswered questions and undeniable inconsistencies; when they have simply become bone-weary; unable to hear another "brand new" revelation, they will lend their voices to the cry of King Solomon: "Vanity of vanity; all is vanity!" (Or, "a chasing of the wind")

But in contrast, the spiritually-awakened (or; ***born again***) are ***qualified to receive divine insights concerning the reality of life.*** Man, made in the image and after the likeness of God is as indefinable as God. That is why his quest should be not to define or categorize himself, but to know his purpose and his duty to God who brought him into being for His own divine purpose.

Even as God will be what he will be, so man also, (as God permits or decrees,) will be what he will be. This too, is "image and likeness." Modern man has tread on foot the surface of the same moon that ancient man gazed upon with wonder and amazement. What indeed is man?

Those who cannot arrive at the truth about the meaning of life can *never* ascertain their own true purpose?

Well, the wisdom imparted thru the writings of King Solomon and the story of his life are given to ultimately lead us beyond their discussions to an even greater truth about life; something simple yet more profound than all the worldly wisdom he had accrued over a lifetime. Do you know what that is?

If you have "an ear (singular) to hear", our Lord Jesus Christ provides us with the answer in Matthew 6 28 & 29.

(28) ... "Consider the lilies of the field, how they grow; they toil not, neither do they spin:

(29) And yet I say unto you, that even Solomon in all his glory was not arrayed like one of these."

Jesus takes the entire magnificent kingdom of Israel raised up through the great wisdom and leadership of king Solomon and compares the glory of it all, not to a field of lilies, but just one single lily and declares that Solomon in all his glory, could not be compared with the glory that was upon one of those lilies.

But here is the spiritual message of the passage:

The real comparison is between the glory of Solomon and the glory of God; not the glory of the lily, but the glory of him who "creates" lilies and glorifies them by "clothing" them to manifest His own purpose. This is what it means to be "clothed" with glory by God.

The former is the works of the hands of men; the latter is wrought by the hand of God.

So then, **the God-given glory bestowed upon the lily was greater than all the wealth, fame, and power of King Solomon.** *Thus, the most powerful man in the world of that time cries out: "Vanity of vanities; all is vanity and vexation of spirit!" Look at Ecclesiastes 2 11: "Then I looked on all the works that <u>my hands</u> had wrought, and on the labor that <u>I</u> had labored to do: and, behold, all was vanity and vexation of spirit, and there was no profit under the sun.*

God alone creates all things and determines their value. Man can create nothing. The best he can do is "make" from borrowed materials, for the earth is the Lord's and the fullness thereof; the world and they that dwell therein.

Man, the creature, cannot claim true ownership of anything including his own self.

So then, we understand that ***Jesus was not comparing the glory of Solomon's life with the glory of the life of a simple lily, but rather, the incomparable glory of God who "clothed" the lily and formed it for His own purpose.***

The clear lesson here is that having the glory of God on one's life is far greater than any glory that one can ever attain through his or her own efforts. Man's highest glory is found in living out the days of his temporary life in the favorable will of God.

Now if any of us accept for ourselves the explanation of life as presented by King Solomon in the book of Ecclesiastes as our "philosophical template", and take counsel of him through all the books he has written, we will certainly gain many valuable insights for living out our "pointless days" on earth. If this is your choice, then "Vanity" is the title inscribed upon the banner you raise as the definition of your world view. To be sure, in doing so, you will have joined an enormous company of like-minded people whose history goes back to ancient times.

But in subscribing to this life philosophy, you should know the following:

(1) That the books written by King Solomon certainly do not supply us with anything close to full disclosure on the matter of life's meaning and purpose. But seeing this very real aspect of life, the

vanity of the temporal, although not conclusive, is vitally necessary before moving forward.
(2) To embrace them as conclusive is to establish one's view of life and reality based on partial information.

God is clearly referenced in these writings, (Proverbs, Ecclesiastes, and Songs of Solomon). They provide us with practical guidance on how to acknowledge and live wisely before an all-seeing God who will honor your reverence and bless your life in this world.

But there is more to life than the things we have discussed up to this point.

God has provided those of us who believe the inspired words of his messengers, with answers that will not only allow us to make sense out of our existence, but to joyfully anticipate the things to come!

So, what's next? Because you see, there must be a "next"; otherwise, my arrival to, brief stay upon, and departure from this planet will have indeed, become utterly meaningless. This is the "vanity" being articulated in the Psalms and Ecclesiastes.

If there is not a "next", then we all have reason for despair. Hope then, must necessarily acknowledge defeat at the hand of futility. Purpose has vanished without a trace leaving no reason to anticipate its return.

Natural man has embraced many philosophies, but what is the truth?

The reason this subject is of very practical importance is because there is reality and there is unreality and the Bible makes us to know that many have embraced a view of life that is not in accordance with the former but the latter.

Some believe that there is no Creator, which makes life an effect without a cause. However, statistics reveal that most humans continue to believe in a Supreme Being.

The Bible is the only book that unfolds the story of life in such a way that an earnest searcher for truth can discover life's supreme purpose. The inspired word of God points us to our Creator and makes life's meaning clear to all who will receive its simple, all-important love-centered message of fellowship with God and one's neighbor.

Yet, there are many false concepts that have been born and nourished to full maturity and spawned the offspring to new generations of error. There are many theories provided for us by the scientific community on how life began.

There are also, several hundred stories about creation provided by various religious groups around the world. But the truths found in the Bible are the revelations of those things God has chosen to share concerning his eternal plan for all creation.

The Bible says: "In the beginning, God created the heaven and the earth."

I believe the Bible's testimony of creation, as well as all subsequent teachings found within its inspired pages; and it is from this perspective that I have written all that you will read in this book.

But let's be clear that this is not a study on "the origin of life". You see, the books that make up the Bible were not written to focus on the details of the origin of life. That was a matter about which none of its authors were in question. To this very day, the inspiration that produced their writings centuries ago continues to abide in the hearts of those of us who believe. We rejoice in the fact that the Creator has revealed himself to us through their words. This is the reason why for us, life is filled with meaning and purpose.

We do not look to science for our understanding of God. No one should look for answers from a source that was not made to address the questions being asked.

Let me use this example to show you what I mean: The subject of "law" is in the Bible, but I would not use the Bible as my primary reference book to prepare for a career in U.S. law. If I should memorize it from cover to cover, the knowledge acquired would not qualify me to become a U.S. attorney, and I would be foolish to have such an expectation.

Obviously, my point is that scientists should keep doing what scientists do, which is clearly not to teach theology, but to study and learn more about how the material world works.

Many people will rest all their confidence and hope in their findings. This however, I, and those whose faith is centered upon the word of God will not do.

People of faith and spiritual understanding are neither intellectually challenged nor blindly superstitious. We do however; examine all the theories offered by those who study these scientific matters in the light of God's sure revelation. Those theories that eliminate the existence of God are even more quickly eliminated in the hearts of his children, for therein is no "fertile ground" for such bad seeds.

So then, let us leave science to its work. Let the theorists continue to probe for answers. But let the people of faith examine the word of God with the foundational understanding that God is spirit, and that indeed, the essence of life itself is spirit.

And so, from that perspective, let us ask the question again............Life: What is it? Clearly, from what may be observed in nature, or detected by the senses, there is no single definition that will suffice. It is more than existence; it is intelligence, power, ability, and authority; it is activity; it is that which can "be" and "become." But ultimately, life is the unfolding, unalterable, ultimate mind and will of God. It is what has happened, is happening, and WILL HAPPEN.

No matter how life is "humanly" defined, its true definition was revealed to us by the Lord Jesus Christ in these words: "And this is life eternal, that they might know thee the only true God, and Jesus Christ, whom thou hast sent." (John 17 3)

Someone will say here, "Yeah, but that's eternal life Jesus is speaking of". "Aren't we supposed to be talking about life in this world"?

Let me share something with you right here: The truth is that in the non-scriptural strict sense of the word, all life is eternal; or never-ending.

Scripturally-speaking however, no unregenerate person has eternal life which is, in this sense, the very life of God.

Still, I know someone is wondering how I can say that all life is never-ending when people are dying every day. This is because they do not understand life's true nature. Life never transforms from what it is to something else. When people die, life doesn't become death. Life and death are two eternally different matters.

When God made man, he raised him up from the dry soil infusing that soil with sub-atomic, spiritually-empowered particles full of divinely-delegated intelligence. He "breathed" spiritually-saturated oxygen into the nostrils of the man he had formed. God's spirit mingled with the oxygen was the divinely-watered "seed", and man's body, divinely instilled with innate intelligence was the "soil". When the "seed" united with the "soil", conception occurred and the man "became a living soul". The result was that God had created a being that was equipped to enjoy fellowship on two planes of reality; natural and spiritual.

The Bible puts what I just said in much simpler words: "And the LORD GOD formed man of the dust of the ground, and breathed into his nostrils the breath of life; and man became a living soul". (Genesis 2 7)

But man, through disobedience, would suffer death. This is another matter altogether; a SUBJECT that needs to be carefully, prayerfully, and thoughtfully considered BECAUSE: People are equally confused about the true meaning of death. It is not a state of non-existence, but rather, a state of separation.

Perhaps a better way to put it to make my point a little clearer is that death is the state of a thing after something else has departed from it. That departing thing is life.

So then, you see; *life does not turn into death. And death is not a void; or vacuum left after life's departure; it is a presence; a state of existence.* So, do not confuse death with "nothingness" or simply a "vacuum", for death is far from being "nothing". It is in fact, the final enemy of mankind that Christ shall destroy. It is already "under his feet." (1st Corinthians 15 26)

"Nothingness" does not qualify as an enemy, but death does, for once again; *it is a state of existence separated from life.* It is, in fact, the realm of reality that preserves the existence of the souls of those alienated from life.

And even as man is a dual-natured being both natural and spiritual, so is death, both natural and spiritual.

What most don't understand is that it is spiritual death that is the true enemy of man; not the physical death of God's children that Jesus called "sleep."

"Where then, does life go when we experience physical death"; someone will ask? Well, I will answer that question with a question. Where did it come from? If we know this, then we know where it goes, for it returns to its source.

Life is spirit. Life in you or me, is (a) spirit. Don't hurry past that statement or you will miss the significance of it. Now even though the life in man is two-fold; (natural and spiritual) the life force is singular. Oxygen supplies life to the body through the blood, but it is spirit (the substance of God) that supplied life to the oxygenated blood.

That which natural man calls life, according to the word of God contains the element of death because it is under the curse of death caused by sin.

What man deems to be his natural state is more correctly defined as "post-natural". The original "natural" was lost.

Without a spiritual re-birth, man can never perceive that which truly constitutes life.

Look again at the pure definition of life from the words of the Lord Jesus Christ: *"And this is life eternal, that they might know thee, the only true God, and Jesus Christ, whom thou hast sent."* (John 17 3)

It is impossible to rightly understand life without a living relationship with its Author. Indeed, knowledge of, and communion with God is the irrefutable key to understanding the meaning and purpose of life. There are so many who don't understand this.

As we all live out this ongoing experience of natural life genetically passed down to us by the first man, Adam, we also all inherited the curse of death from him. Because of this, mankind lives out natural, physical life in a spiritual state of death; physically alive, but spiritually dead. Instead of being Spirit-led, he is now "flesh-driven. "(Genesis 6 3)

So then, spiritually dead man may naturally learn, grow and flourish, but he does so in a divinely cursed world abiding in a state of spiritual death. A world largely populated with souls whose "spiritual phone lines" have gone "dead" cannot figure out why so many things are so wrong on this earth.

So many have never considered the answers found in the sacred scriptures. Many have been "drawn away" by humanistic theories in which they have placed all their confidence. That is why there are so many who are racing on the treacherous rapids of a life out of control desperately searching for fulfillment in all the wrong people, places or things.

It seems that most people continue to just try to "get a handle" on a grand scheme of things that makes sense out of their existence; some all-encompassing; howbeit, general explanation of life and reality. There are multitudes of people; believers included, who, having experienced many things, are yet unclear about their own purpose in life.

We are conscious of, and intrigued by the matters we experience between birth and death. Volumes have been written to discuss each exclusively because it is the interval between the two, which is certainly the focal point of man's interest if he is to make sense of any of it.

Man has been endowed with the powers of reason and imagination. Through these gifts, he has been able to study the material world around him and his creative abilities seem almost endless. But are they sufficient to eventually lead him to absolute and conclusive answers to the question of life's ultimate meaning? Or maybe, as some "brilliant" theorists suggest…. LIFE has no meaning!!….AND IT'S OVER WHEN IT'S OVER, and that is all we will EVER know for certain!

In the scientific community, those dedicated to the study of this subject have found that a uniform or conclusive definition continues to elude them. A biologist is a scientist dedicated to the study of life, yet scientists can't agree on an absolute definition. Here's the plain truth: Scientists just don't know what life is; or how it came to be. And the most troublesome question for them is —why?

Certainly, people view life in many ways; and from many different perspectives. There are also, many subtle shades of meaning that may be applied. But, however many definitions are available according to the concepts of men, in this writing, we will pursue understanding according to the pure truth of the word of God.

And for those of us who believe, one thing is for certain: Life is unmistakably the content of God's intent and purpose. As should be expected, the scriptures have much to say to us concerning this matter.

The truth is that there are certain matters that are rightly assigned to the world of natural science because they belong to the realm of NATURE.

On the other hand, spiritual matters belong to the realm of SPIRIT and should be investigated there. *Although many people are unaware of this fact, the matter of life at its most rudimentary level is <u>always</u> a matter involving spirit.*

There is the natural and there is the spiritual; the earthly and the heavenly. But clearly, not everyone is qualified to engage in the proper investigation of the mysteries of both realms. Those who are unable to make this distinction have already, by default, been relegated and confined to the realm of the natural. This is because they are natural men and the material world only, is their impassable abode.

The Bible says, "As he thinketh in his heart, so is he." (Proverbs 23 7) Indeed, our "identities" are established based on what we believe in our hearts, but those things of which we "feel" certain do not "produce" reality; only our perception of it.

So then, countless lives are driven by unreality that is perceived to be reality. It is fallen man's "reality" and it is out of harmony with reality as established by God. Man cannot, by himself, ascend to kingdom life; the place of true revelation concerning life.

To transcend to the higher dimension of the spirit where the things of God may be known, Jesus informs us that one must be born again; (or from "above.") "That which is born of spirit is spirit and that which is born of the flesh is flesh" So then, the worldview of the born-again believer is to be founded upon the word of God. We will therefore, search the scriptures, for in them is found the testimony of the truth of life's origin, purpose and destiny.

As I previously stated, this book is based upon the conviction that within the pages of the Holy Bible is found the word of God. It is what I believe, and it is the foundation upon which every proposition put forth in this book rests. Whatever claims are made in this book, they are based on my absolute confidence in the divine integrity of the truths of _that_ book.

CHAPTER 2

Eternity Past

'Before the mountains were brought forth, or ever thou hadst formed the earth and the world, even from everlasting to everlasting, thou art God." (Psalms 90:2)

"From everlasting to everlasting, thou art God", clearly says to us about God that He is without beginning or end". That is to say, that his existence extends *from* time out of mind *to* time out of mind.

The word "everlasting" in the verse comes from the Hebrew word: "olam" or "owlam" which can mean any of the following: long duration, antiquity, futurity, for ever, ever, everlasting, evermore, perpetual, old, ancient, and world.

This verse speaks of the existence of God outside of time; or without beginning or end. And we know that the words: "from" and "to", may be used together to speak of the distance between a beginning point and an ending point.

In this case however, the beginning and ending points are both out of view.

Man has been endowed with the faculty of reason and placed in an environment where the phenomenon of "time" is unceasingly at work. Every recordable event occurs within the scope of time's operation. But eternity past is *before* all beginnings.

There is to be found within the pages of the sacred biblical scriptures many references to the dateless past. Consistently, in each of them, a single truth is expounded. That truth is this: that outside the boundaries of time abides the living God.

Thus, we begin with God plus nothing. It is the appropriate place to begin because before there was time, there was God. And although he is at work *in* time, he is not *of* time, but of eternity.

Time is God's invention; but eternity is not a divine invention; it is an aspect of his being.

When we clearly understand this, we can realize that the existence of God is always in the present tense.

So then, it is also necessary for us to rightly distinguish eternity and time in our thinking, understanding that the former is a quality of his Godhood, while the latter is a utility by which his every purpose and action may be recorded for all eternity.

In distinguishing eternity from time, it becomes clear that any examination of what the scriptures call "the beginning" should be preceded by a consideration of that which was before the beginning. That is why we are examining the subject of eternity past.

Before time there was no heaven, no earth, no universe, no atomic matter; only God abiding alone in his majestic solitude. Counseling with Himself from all eternity, this solitary God, having need of nothing, was free to do all that He determined to do according to his own good pleasure.

He made the worlds because it pleased Him to do so; period.

*And the fact is, His greatness is enhanced by nothing we can ever present to Him; not our worship or praise; nor our sacraments or giving; not our obedience, nor any other thing. Not that these things don't matter to Him; it's just that they add nothing to His exceeding greatness. It is only **we** who stand to gain by these things, for God is always the Benefactor and we, the beneficiaries. That is why our dependence upon Him is the indispensable element required in order that we might please Him. -- "But without faith it is impossible to please him"(Hebrews11 6)*

So then, when we speak of eternity past, we speak of that which cannot be identified or associated with a single beginning. That which is from eternity past existed always, never having begun.

Only God Himself, in all the fullness of His Being, can entirely represent eternity past. He is now, as these words are being uttered, exactly what He was, and will be from eternity to eternity. Concerning himself, he says in *Malachi 3 6* "For I am the LORD, **I change not**... and in James 1 17, "*every good gift and every perfect gift is from above, and cometh down from the* **Father of lights, with whom is no variableness**, *neither shadow of turning.*"

For us, eternity past represents that which was before the beginning of time; and even here, our use of the word, "time" must, for the sake of certainty, be limited in its scope, relating only to those things associated to us in this human dispensation.

The mysteries implicit in the subject of eternity past are legion, and in many regards, humanly incomprehensible.

As for us, from the times of our births, all of us have witnessed the beginning and ending of things. Most of us have, by experience, come to realize that in this life, nothing lasts forever. That is because God created us and placed us in an ever-changing world subject in every way, to the dictates of time.

So then, the natural order of human life accommodates for our minds, the idea of time, and our finite earthly minds can somewhat embrace the concept of "forever". It is because if our lives cease to exist, they seem to have no reason for having ever been.

The concept of "that which never ends however, is far more "palatable" to us than the consideration of that which *is*, yet never had a beginning! Just stop right now on that one!

Don't even bother. It is beyond the limits of human reason. It is far outside of our intellectual jurisdiction!

We are not naive concerning the weightiness of the subject, nor careless regarding the reverential spirit in which we engage it. To be sure, the certainty with which we shall speak of these matters is based on faith in the absolute integrity of the revelation of scripture.

I say to you here and now, that this writer professes to "know" nothing.

All that has been written thus far, and all else that shall be written is according to complete faith in the revelation that God has provided us in the Holy Scriptures.

I must tell you that I am convinced that you also know nothing. For "knowing" in the truest sense, is a purely divine characteristic.

So then, when I say that neither you nor I, know anything, I do not mean that we are mindless fools void of all understanding. It is just that all of our "knowledge is incomplete.

Much of what is "known" today by man's careful scientific research will prove to have been incomplete; or in some cases, inaccurate in the years to come; and most likely, by way of the same system of research.

Too often we have witnessed yesterday's fact become today's folly. We must accept the fact that fallibility is a characteristic that comes along with being human.

In fact, no intelligent creature endowed with the faculty of volition though originally made perfect by its infallible Creator, contained the element of infallibility. The reason why is because infallibility is a purely divine characteristic.

Think about it. If the beings God created were infallible, there could never have been a "fall"; neither Luciferian nor Adamic, because in such a case, failure would have been impossible. It is a fact that he created no free-willed beings; neither man nor angels as infallible beings. Their fallibility came with their power of choice.

Now, consider the consequences of this truth: Through the moral failure of an angelic being called a Cherub, the heavens were corrupted. (Job 4 18 15 5) Through the moral failure of a man, spiritual death occurred in man; but the earth upon which he dwelt was already made subject to the possibility of corruption and decay separate from, and prior to his fall. (Genesis 3 17 thru 19) also, (Romans 8 20)

Science informs us that matter is indestructible, but it fails to provide us with the reason this is so. But the reason is: that all matter is inhabited by the indivisible; indestructible life of God. And God cannot be disunited because he is spirit; the original source and upholding of every existing thing. (Hebrews 1 3) Thusly, he must be distinguished from all he contains and indwells.

We must see that the creation, (while distinct from its Creator), was not endowed with incorruptibility; nor man infallibility.

In Psalms 119 5, David cries: "O that my ways were *directed* to keep your statutes!" (In other words: If only it was automatic!)

Does this mean that none of God's intelligent, free-willed creatures will ever be immune from the possibility of moral failure? Perhaps, but I don't believe it does.

Let's not despair; keep reading.

When Christ was on the earth, all of God's fullness dwelled within him. (Colossians 1 19 and 2 9) This could be said of no other man on earth. But there is coming a time when God will be "all in all". 1ˢᵗ Corinthians 15 28) Perhaps someone is asking: "What does this term, "all in all" mean?

Well, I believe the term points to a future time when all of God's fullness will dwell in all of God's redeemed and glorified creation. Just as Colossians 1:19 tells us that it pleased the Father to dwell in Jesus in all his fullness, so it will be in us.

Then, there shall be no separation. It will be God the Father and the Sons of God; Jesus Christ being the firstborn of many brethren. (Romans 8 29).

At that time, we will all recognize that sonship has nothing to do with gender in the natural sense of the word, for God is neither male nor female. If anybody claims to know what God's glorified children will be, they know more than the Apostle John, who could only say with certainty, that we shall be like Jesus. (1st John 3 2.

That's why he says to the entire congregation of believers; male and female alike: "Beloved, now are we the *sons* of God". This was more than just a form of address customary to the culture. It was a rhema word.

Before this "corruptible" puts on "incorruption" and this "mortal" puts on immortality, none of us, his children know what we shall be. We only know that when he (the Lord Jesus Christ) shall appear, we shall be like him. (1st John 3 2) It is the time God speaks of during which He shall make all things new. (Revelations 21 5)

In this eternal dispensation, it may be said that redeemed man "cannot sin" because he "will not"; perhaps not that he "will not" sin because he "cannot." In that dispensation, it is certain that he is neither willing, nor compelled to do so. I believe that his will to righteousness is reinforced by the eternal remembrance of his redemption.

But for now, man can only know in part. He knows *much* about many things, but he knows *all* about nothing. Endless facts may be obtained through careful and meticulous investigation. Natural truths may be uncovered in a natural world, but *the underlying spiritual truths belong to the spiritual world, and they are not accessible by natural means. These are the unseen "whys" behind the "what's" that the natural man observes.*

The Creator knows with exact certainty; the truth of that which the man of faith believes and knows by steadfast confidence in God's revelation. Knowledge based upon exact certainty understands not only the "what" of a matter, but also the "how" and the "why"; including both original and final intent. If man knew these things, life would not be the mystery that it is.

The word "eternal" refers to an infinite amount of time; lasting forever; continuing without interruption. You see, time does not actually interrupt eternity; it merely identifies the beginning, duration, and end of all phenomena occurring during the course of it.

Now think deeply about this definition of eternity.

When we speak of eternity past, we do so considering our recognition of a divinely-designated "interjection into", or division of, eternity brought on by this introduction of time. It is time that has divided eternity into past and future.

Time is easily distinguished from eternity in that it is defined by having a beginning and an end. It is a marker; a symbol by which any act or expression can be measured.

<u>Eternity</u> is a never-ending stream. <u>Time</u> is a vessel filled with activity sailing on that stream.

Time is related to activity; all activity. Activity is related to power. Without power, there is no activity. Every act of God is also an expression of His power. Every act of every living creature is also, an expression of God-given power. Every act began at some point. That point is a point in time. Whenever the activity ceases, another point in time has been established.

God has predetermined and foreordained before each "time" began, that certain things come to pass during that time. He has declared the immutability of the outcome of all He has purposed to do.

There is a divine plan that God saw as finished before He ever began, because once God conceives a thing, it is! When the thing materializes before the creature, it is merely a delayed occurrence of that which God already witnessed.

He has placed us humans in this realm of time and allotted each one of us a space of it. He has given us life, ability, time, and the power of choice. Now why do you suppose He has done this? <u>**It is for us to ultimately awaken to His divine purpose for our lives. He desires that by our own free wills, we submit to His will in order that we might spend eternity in glorious fellowship with Him.**</u>

Listen closely: He became one <u>of</u> us so that all of us could become one <u>in</u> Him. (Jesus said: "I and my Father are one."(John 10 30) He also prayed to the Father that we all may be one in him and the Father. (John 17 21)

From eternity past, God decreed that *there would be a remnant of people set apart* from among the human family who through His Son would become His family.

But from eternity past, He has neither randomly, nor arbitrarily chosen any of us *as individuals* to be saved.

Please understand that: none of us *individually* represent His Elect; His Chosen. This distinction belongs singularly, to His only-begotten Son. We are however, His elect *in* the Son. There is no favor with God possible among men apart from the Son. (Acts 4 12)

The Elect of God

Christ is God's Elect; (Isaiah 42 1) His Chosen One, (Matthew 12 18) and all believers were foreknown as a pre-determined class of humanity *in Him* so that we, *in Him*, are God's elect; His chosen; not as individuals, but as **a class of humans known in scripture as the "Church"**. (Ephesians 1 4)

The "Elect;" or election of God is a pre-determined category, or class of people whose foreordained destiny is to be conformed to the image of the Son. (Romans 8 29)

Once again, these are not individually selected persons that God has predestined and irresistibly drawn into that class; **it is *the class itself* that God has predestined**. Those who make up that class have met the conditions of *a right response to the gospel message.*

Also, those angels who demonstrated probity by maintaining their integrity at the time of the angelic rebellion are called the elect angels. These may also include angels assigned to higher rank such as Michael and Gabriel.

From eternity past, God foreknew all that He Himself would bring to pass, but He also foresaw all that His free-willed creatures would do. He did not pre-determine the actions of His free-willed creatures, but He did predetermine the *consequences* of those actions. In theological terms, it is commonly called the "the law of sowing and reaping."

We must be clear about the fact that God foresaw from eternity, much that He did not personally cause to occur in this "going forth" of the Word of God; this dispensation, age, or the realm of time. *In this realm of time, there are many wills at work.* Nonetheless, only an infinitely sovereign God can preside over, and determine the boundaries of all possibility. And because this is true, the full will of the creature can only be exercised within space allotted to him by his Maker. Simply put: God is eternally in control of all things.

In the beginning, God said, "Let there be; and there was. At some point, He said, "Let us make man in our own image and after our own likeness." It was at that point that another free will was "authorized" to exist on the earth. But there were free-willed beings whose abode was upon the earth as well as in the heavenlies even before this. In fact; before the earth existed at all, there were already free-willed beings.

But until some point in eternity past, there was only one will at work. It was the perfect will of God.

Surely the question must come to mind, "With so many wills at work, how could God be assured that all He intended to come to pass would happen unless He made it to be so?" Well, the simple answer is that He *is* making all His purpose to come to pass, and He is doing so without overriding man's free will, unless of course, he chooses to.

So then, in summary, what may be learned from all this?

Well, firstly, we see that from eternity past through time and into eternity future, God has an immutable plan that includes humanity.

We also know that when God created angels and men, He made them not flawed, but fallible and gave them free will. From this fact, we realize that it is quite possible for things to occur in the realm of time that are not according the *divine will*, but the will of the creature by *divine permission*.

Perhaps someone's understanding about the current state of the world is being enlightened by the consideration of these facts.

As we proceed, we will begin to see the unfolding revelation of His grand purpose which is not exclusively about us, but includes us...

God, knowing that there could be no other Him, determined that He would make images and likenesses; representations or expressions of Himself. And as we consider the vast, seemingly infinite expanse of the universe and ascribe its design and creation to God, to say that we lowly vessels of clay are in His image and likeness seems absurd. But God seems to love to express the greatness of His power and love through the humble and lowly things of this world. It is why Jesus encourages us to consider the lilies of the field, or the sparrows. Based on the word of the Lord, we know that our finite minds operate according to a pattern that emulates (on an infinitesimally smaller scale) the infinite mind of God.

The scriptures tell us that we may discover much about God's nature by studying the things He has made.

Now if we ourselves are made in His image and after His likeness, then it is within ourselves that the revealed truth about His divine nature shall be manifested. This means that as God reveals Himself in us, His will and purpose for our lives shall also be revealed.

Those who are seeking God and His kingdom outside of themselves have not understood that the rulership of God within us is the only means by which God can manifest His good will and purpose for our lives.

Even as we understand that replicas and pictures do not possess physical life, so we must understand that we can never be the images of God except His life, which is Spirit, abides in us. And we can never be after the likeness of God unless He is able by His Spirit, to express Himself through us. The simple fact is a great revelation that each of us was created to be little expressions of God. Every material thing on earth is an expression of His *purpose*, but only man is the earthly expression of His *Person*.

Here is a profound truth expressed in simplicity: God alone is life; the Word of God is life personified; and everything

He created and made was designed to be an expression of His purpose. This is indeed, life's purpose.

Not everything is an expression of God, but everything is in its original, uncorrupted state, an expression of His will and purpose.

Please note however, that man was uniquely designed to be a particular expression of God. Thus, He was made "in the image and after the likeness" of God.

In a serenely simple word, the true story of life is about a Divine Father and His Family.

So, with this summary understanding, let us move forward from the subject of eternity past to the scriptural resources God has provided to reveal what He would have us to know about the beginning.

CHAPTER 3

The Beginning

Genesis 1:1 says: "In the beginning, God created the heaven and the earth."

This statement seems to be straightforward. At a glance, there seems to be nothing in it to encourage us to linger here. But perhaps there is more here than can be recognized in a quick glance.

For example: what beginning? Is this opening verse referring to the beginning of time? It seems that it must be, for it identifies the 1st reference to God at work, thus, it appears that the original advent and procession of time should be simultaneous with the 1st revealed and recorded act of God. It clearly isn't referring to the beginning of human or animal life since they didn't come into existence until days 5 and 6 after God created the heaven and the earth.

And then, what was meant by the terms: "morning", "evening", and "day"? Were the first 5 verses in Genesis the beginning and conclusion of the 1ˢᵗ 24-hour day? If the statement in verse 1 refers to the beginning of time, are we to believe that this beginning marks the start of 24-hour solar days?

If one believes this, can this view be scripturally proven, or even logically assumed? Is the reference to morning and evening at the end of each creative day synonymous with the days, nights, seasons, and years that are governed by the sun and the moon, as it is said in Genesis 1:14? Or, do these terms clearly speak of different matters? I certainly believe in the latter consideration.

It seems that we might safely say that verse 1 refers to the beginning of the creative operation of God. After all, the word "beginning" is associated with the word "created".

Okay. Good; but now let's adjust the question slightly so that you can get the full scope of what I am asking. So now, instead of asking "what beginning", let me ask you "which" beginning? Is the beginning in this verse the beginning of all beginnings? If one believes it is, my question once again is: Is this idea scripturally provable?

I trust that by now, some have been persuaded to consider that this reference to "the beginning", in fact, to the entire creation story is not quite as straightforward as can be clearly understood with a quick glance. Fact is, that is the nature of the search for truth.

Then the verse goes on to say that God created the heaven and the earth…. again, not nearly as straightforward as it appears at first glance. Which heaven? The Bible speaks of heaven in both the singular and the plural, and clearly, there is more than one heaven. All the biblical references to heaven are clearly not speaking of the same place.

And then again; are we even clear about which earth? Because among believers, myself included, there are many that believe the creation story, as it unfolds in the verses following verse 1, are a break from verse 1 and begins a new narrative; a narrative that is describing the restoration of an earth that had a much earlier history; one that began and ended catastrophically at the end of that 1st verse.

To be sure, there is scriptural support to back these considerations, and as we move forward, we will examine them.

There is much to be learned about God in this book of Genesis. The God-inspired scriptures testify and reveal secret things about him to those of us who seek with our whole hearts.

Now consider a little further with me if you will, the concept of "*beginnings*" as found in scripture. Please understand that there is more than one singular all-inclusive event identified in the word of God as a "beginning".

To this fact, I raise the following question:

Is this beginning found in the 1st verse of the first book of the Bible *indisputably __THE__ Beginning of __all__ beginnings*; or simply *__THE__ beginning for us*? Or, is this reality, one of many divine dispensations framed by time and marked off by what is called "the beginning and the ending?"

Psalms 93 2 says: "Thy throne is established of old: thou art from everlasting." Now please listen closely: Only God knows how many *times;* (dispensations of time) there have been. As far as we know, the number of them is infinite. Can this consideration be disputed based upon scriptural evidence?

Perhaps many of us have given little or no thought to the fact that the eternal mind of the eternal God has been at work from all eternity.

Some may reply: "Perhaps not, and so what?"

My answer to them would be that in not having done so, certain mistaken assumptions may be established in their thinking about the full scope of what is meant by "the beginning." His activities from the dateless past are described by the prophet Micah (Micah 5 2) as His *"goings forth."* There can be no question as to whom Micah is referring: "But thou, Bethlehem Ephratah, though thou be little among the thousands of Judah, yet out of thee shall he come forth unto me that is to be ruler in Israel; *whose goings forth have been from of old, from everlasting.* We are considering eternity past.

The person who would be born in Bethlehem of the tribe of Judah is an eternal, uncreated being who has been "going forth" (plural) from all eternity.

As a man, He came into being. He had a beginning and was born into the world; but *as God*, He had neither birth nor origin.

As a man, He is the <u>Son of God</u>. We now know Him as Jesus Christ.

As God, He is the <u>eternal Word</u>; never called in scripture God's "eternal" son. This fact helps us to understand why there is no divine father and son relationship heard of in the entire Old Testament. Apart from prophecy, it is only after Jesus is born into the world and reaches the age of twelve that we hear of it. (Luke 2 49) He is God's only begotten (*or, divinely; supernaturally born*) son.

He was also, by divine operation, the son of Mary, who was at the time of his birth, a virgin through whom he received his humanity. He did not inherit Mary's sin nature as she was honored to only be the repository of the coming child who was Himself, ***eternal life*** personified.

<u>In his divinity</u>, he is the Word of God; <u>in his humanity</u>, he is God's son, and after the flesh, Mary's son.

Mary, who was clearly a godly young maiden, neither *is*, nor *was* divine. She is not (as erroneously proclaimed by many) the "mother of God." Nor should she still be called "the virgin" as she and Joseph married and had several other sons and daughters. In Mark 6:3, we learned that Jesus had at least 4 half-brothers and 2 half-sisters.

Mary was a chosen vessel; godly yet inherently, thru Adam, possessing a sin-nature. This however, would not be passed on to the "holy thing" that she, thru divine operation, would give birth to.

So then, by way of the Holy Spirit, eternal life was transplanted from heaven into the womb of the virgin girl. In the operation of this divine process, God's Spirit would extract from Mary every sinless element of her humanity for the formation of the body that would be the habitation of God.

According to His divine nature, He is identified by the Apostle John as the Word. (John 1 1) It is He, whose "goings forth" have been from "of old" as noted by the prophet Micah. He is the Word of God; that is His divine identity. (Revelation 19 13)

So, as we prepare to move forward to examine what the Bible has to say about the subject of "the beginning," let us bear in mind this fact: It is (*this*) beginning and (*this*) end in (*this*) divinely-ordained space of time with which we finite creatures must be concerned. Now; let's go to the "Beginning" found in Genesis 1 1. Here, it says: "In the beginning, God created the heaven and the earth." Right here, let us take this single passage and isolate it as though it was a completed discussion of the subject; because, as I said before, it is. (Just stay with me.)

Let me ask you. Do you casually take it for granted that God did all this creative work over the course of six 24-hour days? I did!

In fact, I had read those three words several times over the years without entertaining any different or deeper consideration of the words that followed concerning His six days of work.

I learned over the years that the sacred scriptures are not just given to us to read; nor are they merely to be memorized; but they are to be meditated upon. In Psalms 1:2, David identified one of the practices of the blessed man saying that "In His (God's) law doth he meditate day and night."

Now listen closely:

Today, I know that there is no reference to solar days involved in this discussion of the span of time God used to complete creation. Most historians credit the Egyptians with the development of the solar day around 1500 BC. Many Bible scholars try to make that reference to the word ("day") to God's use of the word ("day"). Well, let's see if that is scripturally accurate.

Let me start by asking: Do you believe that the **Day of the Lord** is a 24- hour day? If so, the scriptures prove that to be a mistaken view. Fact is, the Day of the Lord is a span of time during which God personally intervenes in history directly with angelic representation to accomplish some divinely-scheduled purpose. The day should not be examined in terms of hours and minutes, but rather, as the identification of his divinely predestined set of events, the duration of which, is not disclosed to us.

When Jesus said he would raise up the believers "at the **last** day" was he announcing the **end** of the 24-hour day? Would there be no more 24-hour days after that day?

Why should we not take literally the words of Peter in 2nd Peter 3 8: "…. A day with the Lord is as a thousand years, and a thousand years as a day"? Why would God; the Eternal Being use time in the same manner as we time-dependent humans. He gave us the sun, the moon, seasons, day & night for us to use to accomplish our purposes, but he does not confine himself inside those boundaries. He has kept all times and seasons within his own power (read Acts 1 7)

I believe that the mornings and evenings in Genesis regarding creation, refer to the start and finish of each aspect of his creative work, having nothing to do with solar days. Solar days, developed by the Egyptians 4500 years later, were given to be used by man, but God's activity cannot be contained by them.

Who can scripturally prove that the first three words in Genesis 1 represent the beginning of all beginnings. Just because many believe it to be the *first* beginning doesn't necessarily make it so. There is however, sufficient scriptural proof to reveal to us that there have been many beginnings and endings before the age of man. We must remember that not every scriptural reference to the early events of creation relate to man. After all; heaven came first; but even more specific; the unseen, spiritual; then the visible, natural.

Listen closely again, because I will review what I just said plainly:

Creation began *long before* there was any such thing as "*solar days.*" Even in Genesis, the sun appears on the 4th day, helping us to understand that the days made up of evening and morning were not referring to the solar days which God gave humans as a means of measuring time.

God is not earth-bound and we have no scriptural reason to believe that He used the same means of measuring time to accomplish His purpose.

In fact, we have scriptural reason to believe that He did not. Psalms 90 4 says: **"For a thousand years in thy sight are but as yesterday when it is past, and as a watch in the night."**

Jesus said as much to his disciples during his meeting with them after his resurrection in Acts 1 7. He said: "It is not for you to know the times or the seasons, which the Father hath put in his **own** power."

Jesus is obviously not referring to the *natural* **times** and *seasons* in that **Genesis 1 14 says that God gave us the sun and the moon *as a means of knowing* those very things.**

Jesus was talking about the divine "times and seasons" of the fulfilling of His Father's eternal purpose.

It is certain also, that there have been ages or generations prior to the creation of our world about which we know little or nothing.

For example, what is the glory which Jesus refers to having had with the Father before the world was?

Receive this pure scriptural revelation:

It was the glory of being the express image, or representation of the Supreme Being (Hebrews 1 3).

This points to a time or age that pre-dates the present age or generation.

Angels, cherubim, and the entire existing heavenly host were certainly worshipping Him <u>before</u> the events of Genesis 1:2 through 2:3.

How many times in eternity past has the eternal God expressed Himself?

I ask you, how many "beginnings" have there been? How many more will there be?

The Apostle John informs us in Revelations 21 that he saw a new heaven and a new earth, and that the first heaven and the first earth had passed away.

We need not think that because God has spoken to us about the beginning and the end of **this age** that he is no longer thinking, feeling, desiring, determining, decreeing and bringing to pass that which shall be predetermined and foreordained before another "beginning."

Remember Micah 5 2 that was referenced earlier? It says this: *"But thou, Bethlehem Ephratah, though thou be little among the thousands of Judah, yet out of thee shall he come forth unto me that is to be ruler in Israel; whose <u>goings forth</u> have been from of old, <u>from everlasting</u>.*

The plural "goings forth" provide for us clear scriptural reason to believe that there have been countless beginnings and endings; i.e.; "goings forth" prior to the one that marked the beginning of our world.

If our world is (as it has been widely taught in Christian circles) only around six thousand years young, then the creation of it couldn't possibly mark the beginning of the operations (or "goings forth") of the one spoken of in the prophecy in Micah 5 2. There is a great deal of difference between six thousand years ago and "from everlasting."

Genesis 1 1 says: "In the beginning God created the heaven (singular) and the earth." It is significant that "the heaven" is singular here. The use of this word here is the same throughout the book of Genesis. But this word "heaven" is found in the plural; (heavens) three times in Genesis all in chapter two (verses 1 and 4).

Now if you, like me, do not believe that God was creating the entire universe within six 24-hour days in the first chapter of Genesis, then when did He create all the other planets, galaxies, suns and moons; and over how long a period of time? The answer is that no one knows the answer to that question for certain, but 6,000 years ago is definitely not the answer.

When Genesis 1 1 speaks of "the heaven", are we to believe that this reference is synonymous with the plural references found in 2 1 & 4? The answer is: no, we are not. To do so would lead us into scriptural contradiction.

Let's examine the wording found in Genesis 2 1 thru 4:

1. Thus the heavens and the earth were finished, and all the host of them.
2. And on the seventh day God ended his work which he had made; and he rested on the seventh day from all his work which he had made.
3. And God blessed the seventh day, and sanctified it: because that in it he had rested from all his work which God *created* and *made.*
4. These are the generations of the heavens and of the earth when they were created, in the day that the LORD God made the earth and the heavens.

These verses tell us a great deal if we study them carefully. The fact that the word "heaven" is plural (heavens) in these verses as opposed to its singular use in the 1st chapter is significant. What we have in these four verses is a summary of the creative acts of God in which much of their details are undisclosed.

That there were stages of Gods creative work that, concerning time; have absolutely nothing to do with 24-hour days is beyond speculation.

It is also clear that God created the spirit world *before* He created the earth because angelic beings celebrated with singing and shouting when He completed the earth. (Job 38 4 thru 7) They already existed and were eyewitnesses to the handiwork of God. It may very well be that they were also participants in the processing of the divine purpose at God's direction and command! After all, in verse 6, concerning the completion of the earth, God puts forth the question to Job: "(Who) laid the corner stone thereof? .... Who indeed?

At any rate, what we are clear about is that the six days of Genesis 1 are the final days of God's creative operations throughout the entire earthly and celestial universe. That is why in verse 4 the author calls these the "generations" of the heavens and of the earth "when they were created."

So then, Genesis 1 clearly understood, points us not only to what God began but also to what He completed! So, he blessed and sanctified the seventh day and declared it for Himself as a day of rest; the seeds of all His creative purposes implanted in the realms of time and space.

Based upon this understanding, one thing is clear and reiterated. If the "beginning" spoken of in Genesis 1 1 represents the point in eternity past where God first began His creative work, it did not start and finish within six 24-hour days. Yet, in verse 4 of the 2nd chapter, it speaks singularly of **the "day"** that the LORD God made the earth and the heavens.

Let's read verse 4 in the KJV: "These are the *generations (plural)* of the heavens and of the earth when they were created, in the *day* that the Lord God made the earth and the heaven (singular).

So, according to the 4th verse, did He do it all in a day? Are the generations and the heavens spoken of in the first part of the verse referring to a single day? If so, how do we make sense out of the events that occurred in Genesis 1?

Did he complete all his creative activity in a "day"; a generation; or six 24-hour days?

Of course, none of these answers are correct!

The truth is that he performed all his creative work over several generations, and we have no way of knowing with certainty, what should be understood by "the heavens" in this specific context. It seems clear however, that the latter part of the verse is referring to the six creative days (or generations) described in the 1st chapter that refers to the world of humanity.

Anyone could attempt to offer the seemingly irrefutable argument that God, in His omnipotence could have instantaneously completed all His creative works. The point is not whether He could have, but whether He did. And neither the six days of uncertain duration found in this chapter or the description found in Job 38 4 thru 7 support this argument. Clearly, there are no solar days before the appearance of the sun?

And if these six days __did__ represent the original creation of the earth, how long did it take God to finish creating the entire infinite universe of stars, planets, and galaxies which came first, and for which no time is accounted in scripture?

Yet, the first verse of Genesis 1 says they were all created "in the beginning"; or within the same space; or epoch of time? Considering all these things, once again, the questions I ask is *not what __could__ He have done*; but *what __did__ He do*?

In 2 4, Moses says: "These are the *generations* of the heavens and of the earth when they were created, in the day that the LORD God made the earth and the heavens; in other words, this is the history. In this verse, notice that it begins with the generations of the heavens and of the earth.

The order is first the heavens then, the earth when they were created; not made.

But then, in the same verse, the order changes and a specific "day" is cited and it is also here that we have our first reference to the LORD God; or (Yahweh God). This is all significant. In the second part of the verse, the earth is spoken of, then the heavens.

There is a reason why the description of the first part of the verse is different from that of the latter. It is because the entire verse references more than one creative generation and includes a specific point of discussion described as a "day."

"These are the generations"-beginning sometime in the dateless past with the heavens first and then, the earth. All throughout the first chapter, the Creator is simply called "God." Why is he not called the LORD God? (Or Yahweh Adonai)

It is because with God, creation occurs with divine conception. When His thoughts materialized out of nothing but the authority of His Word, He began His use of both spirit and matter to create habitats before He created beings to inhabit them. At that point, there were no beings over whom He could be LORD, for He had not yet created them. But He would do so and call them "sons of God" before He would make the earth.

He who called from nothing that which came into being is God, the Creator.

He who takes of that which He has created and "makes" is the LORD God.

God, our Creator and the LORD God, our Maker is one and the same.

After verse 4, he begins to make it clear that the events spoken of during the six days of chapter 1 represent beginnings to developing and ongoing processes. The "divine seeds" of nature existed before they had been implanted within the earth and were already endowed with reproductive empowerment; all things "after their own kind" according to God's decree. When He spoke, it was!

Remember when I asked you to isolate the first verse of Genesis 1 from the following verses? Let's go back there now.

In the second verse of chapter one, it says that the earth was an empty, formless mass inundated with water and covered in darkness, and that the Spirit of God was moving; or hovering over the face of the waters. Then, God said: "Let there be light." Please understand here, that while the light that appeared at God's command provided illumination, *it was not merely natural light from a natural light source.* (That would appear on the 4th day.)

This "Light" was the "going forth" of the Word of God out from the unapproachable, supernatural light of the Omnipresent God. (1st Timothy 6 16)

That is why when he came down from heaven to earth and became a man, he said: "I Am the Light of the world." It is the reason why there will be no need for the sun in the new earth, for there too, the Lamb will be the Light. (Revelations 21)

To be sure; there will be at that time, a new heaven and a new earth; for this present heaven and earth will have passed away, and he whose "goings forth" are "from everlasting" will be "the Beginning" of yet another beginning.

What shall ultimately and unalterably come to pass concerning our futures is of eternal consequence.

We are moving through time into eternity. But more personally, and more specifically, we, as individuals, are moving through our allotted times, and these borrowed lives must one day, be surrendered up. There will be no more exercising of the free will supposedly independent of the divine will, for the "spirit of rebellion" will exist no more. The redeemed will be freely willing to do the will of the Father.

It is desire that moves the will of man. When we desire the will of God, we will be "filled" with it. It is the "hunger and thirst of which Jesus spoke. In that state, there is, as there has always truly been; only one independent will at work. It is the will of the Divine Judge of all men; Him to whom all souls belong.

If we have been born again and have received the gift of eternal life, it means that we have received the uncreated life of God Himself; as an unconditional possession by way of regeneration thru faith.

Please be clear about this fact: Our <u>eternal security</u> is resting on the foundation of our <u>abiding faith</u> in God. There is truly no way to fathom the everlasting and inconceivable consequences of having entered into such an experience. It will be good for those who in departing from this life, can confidently say: "I have finished my course; I have kept the faith, and it is well with my soul.

There is a saying among men that time changes things, but this is not true. It is true however, that things change in the process of time, but it is not time itself that brings about change.

Time is simply a point of reference by which we may identify and evaluate a range and variety of activities, choices, and changes that occur because of them. The wise king Solomon said: "There is a season and a time for all things; a time to be born and a time to die; a time to sow and a time to reap, etc.; It is this wisdom that admonishes us that we should place a high premium on our time here in this brief life. Time is not subject to us, but we are subject to it.

Time has served the Creator at "designated points" from all eternity and He is never in a hurry because time is His servant. The eternal God has an endless supply of time.

But we are not God. There are time-based constraints placed upon each of us, and it is quite possible for us to miss our time to accomplish certain meaningful and necessary things within the scope of our allotted tenure in this world.

God, in His foreknowledge and determinate counsel, has foreordained and decreed certain things to come to pass in this particular span of time. It is time as it relates to the eternal plan and purpose of God regarding humanity.

Please note that there are no points in time that give reference to the determinate counsels of God, for time itself is a product of such counsel. Foreknowledge is what God knows not during time, but before time begins.

Had he come to know it eventually during time, such would indicate that He is not truly all- knowing; omniscient.

The "determinate counsels" of God have occurred beyond this realm of time throughout eternity past. In other words, from eternity, God has reasoned; or counseled with Himself. He will continue to do the same throughout all eternity. Eternity has been filled with the intellectual activity of the God who imagined, reasoned, desired, determined, decreed, and is performing the fulfillment of all that He has purposed in His heart to do. He foreknew and predestinated all that He is pleased to bring to pass. It is important to understand this truth:

Every act of God is a "going forth" of the Word of God; for *the Word that was made flesh has always, (from eternity) been the express image of God's person.* (Hebrews 1 3) <u>That is why those who had **seen** Jesus had **seen** the Father</u> (John 14 9) because God was in Christ reconciling the world unto himself. (2nd Corinthians 5:19)

CHAPTER 4

Reality Versus Unreality

Reality is the true state of things as they exist. Unreality, on the other hand, is the quality of being imaginary, illusory, or unrealistic.

In our world, we are constantly exposed to falsehood; sometimes, when we are not seeking anything, and then at other times, when we are earnestly seeking the truth. Lies conceal truth, and all have suffered in some way from the effects of a lie.

Who among us has never lied or been lied to? Lying is a spiritual "pandemic" of worldwide proportion. The only thing real about a lie is that it is really a lie. Unreality is any distorted version of the truth.

It is ironic to note that sometimes, deceived unbelievers unwittingly enable their own deceivers to entrench them more deeply in sinful behavior by willfully choosing certain actions. Certainly, born-again people as well, often yield to the impulse to do or say things without regard to the inward alert of their consciences. In so doing, they sometimes expose themselves to unnecessary pressures to be dishonest. In such cases, it cannot be truthfully said that the believer was "led" into temptation; nor did he "fall" into it, but he "entered" it. In so doing, he entered a region of spiritual darkness; where there is no understanding of spiritual things. This is the place in man where the conscience may be over-ridden, and the light of God has been turned off.

But there is a difference between the children of light (born-again believers), and the children of darkness (descendants of Adam). Unregenerate souls are "at home" in the darkness, even as believers once were before being saved.

All who are deceived, believer and non-believer alike, have personal unseen deceivers. All humans have unseen; indeed, invisible adversaries who are not dismissed by one's disbelief. It is in fact, the disbelief in this unseen activity that makes it so effective in deceiving the spiritually blind. Sinful temptation finds the human heart as "fertile soil" for man's pride and lust to flourish.

Along with unconstrained lusts, egotism is a blindfold that causes so much moral turpitude. Jesus said they may see, but they will not perceive; they may hear, but they will not understand. -Mark 4:12. And why is that so? The answer is that God has allowed the enemy to shield proud, unbelieving hearts from seeing the truth.

Our perceptions are established according to our reasonings, but all our reason-based perceptions are subject to error.

Many things in our world appear to many to be something that they actually are not. Many people embrace simple unverifiable explanations for complex matters. Conspiracy theories abound in our world. Important matters that warrant our attention may be overlooked as we gaze hypnotically at things that are in truth, useless distortions of reality. There so many thoughtless opinions freely shared among men, often without any consideration of the possible harm that could result from them.

The Bible tells us that there is a way that seems right to us that is not real and leads to death. (Proverbs 14:12), and that whatever we know, we only know in part; and none of us possesses exhaustive or ***absolute knowledge*** of anything. (1ˢᵗ Corinthians 8:2 & 13:8 thru 9) This is because: absolute knowledge is a divine attribute; a God-quality. What thing do you think you know so well that there is absolutely, without question, nothing that could be added to your body of knowledge? We don't even fully know our own hearts. In Jeremiah 17:9, the Prophet says: "the heart is deceitful above all things and desperately wicked. Who can know it?"

For the entire human family, life is filled with both uncertainty and possibility. These conditions seem to clearly lead us to the inevitable conclusion that this phenomenon we call life is an ever-unfolding mystery. All that we know now is partial and incomplete. Even prophecy only reveals part of the whole picture. (1ˢᵗ Corinthians 13:9 &10.)

But we are here, and we are conscious of our own being, and the existence of the world outside of ourselves because of our moment to moment experiences called "living."

We experience life until we die. That's the simple fact. But it does not automatically follow that we rightly understand what life is, nor its purpose or destiny. I submit to you that none of us really know what life is, apart from God's revelation. And clearly, I say to you that no one in this age has full disclosure. Indeed, as the Apostle Paul said: "We see thru a glass darkly." All human knowledge is progressive, partial, imperfect, and finite. Uncertainty is woven into the fabric of human experience. The Apostle said in 1st Corinthians 8:2 "If anyone supposes that he knows anything, he has not yet known as he ought to know. Some people think before they speak. Some exercise very little thought. Many popular sayings are false. Many false things seem right to shallow thinkers, and many wrong conclusions have been arrived at by those who think deeply. These are they who build a case for their idea not realizing that they started from a wrong premise.

To illustrate my point, I will ask: How many times have you heard someone say concerning all people that "We are all God's children? Many times, in my life, I have heard people say this. But is that the truth? Is that what the Bible teaches? I didn't ask you if that was what the reverend said! Tell me; is Romans 1:18 referring to God's children? Let's read what it says: "For the wrath of God is revealed from heaven against all ungodliness and unrighteousness of men, who by their unrighteousness, suppress the truth." God has never, and will never pour out his wrath upon his children. There is coming, a day of wrath, and God's children are clearly not a part of it.

But rather, Colossians 3:6 tells us that the wrath of God is going to come on the children of disobedience. These are the same as those in Romans 1:18 who by their unrighteousness, suppress the truth. Whose children are these? God's? No, they are not! They are the devil's children, and as Jesus said: "His works they will do. (John 8:44)

How about this one.... "God loves everybody" …. Says who? That is certainly not what the Bible says. Do you really think that God loves without distinction? Such an idea is mythical. Nor can such an idea be corroborated by scripture. Does God love the wicked as well as the righteous? Does he love those who hate him? Well, let's see what the scriptures have to say about these matters.

Psalms 11:5 NLT says: "The LORD examines both the righteous and the wicked. He HATES those who love violence." This verse alone proves that God searches the hearts of men and distinguishes the right intentions of those he calls "the righteous" from the wicked thoughts and intentions of unrepentant willfully evil people. Those are the people he hates. He doesn't just hate the violence; he hates the people who love the violence. He hates those who have no regard for morality; who practice iniquity. (Psalms 5:5) He hates slandering liars and all who cause strife and division. (Proverbs 6:19). He examines and hates their thoughts (Proverbs 15:26), He hates their worship (15:8), and he hates their actions (6:18) So, it is clear, that if someone wants to make a case for the proposition that God loves everybody, that person cannot use the Bible to prove it.

But let us also, be clear about this fact: The God who is love, takes no pleasure in the fact that the wicked ARE wicked. Twice in the book of Ezekiel he says he finds no pleasure in the death of the wicked; and that he desires to see the wicked turn from his ways. (Ezekiel 18:32 & 33:11) He is ever ready to receive any soul that turns from the evil, and comes to him.

But God hates wickedness, and if, in his sight, any person becomes the embodiment of wickedness, that person has become an object of God's hate. He does not distinguish and separate the rebel from his rebellion. How does he punish the rebellion and leave the rebel unpunished? We identify a liar by the lies he tells. What he says flows from what is in his heart. If God loves liars, why is he going to send them all into the lake of fire? (Revelations 1:8)

If a person commits murder, can murder be incarcerated or executed, and the murderer go free? But we must not think of God's hatred as if it were an emotional thing. We must understand that the unchanging God of all creation; the Lord God first spoken of in Genesis, is the unchanging God with us, in the person of Jesus Christ. His hatred is perfectly integrated with all the rest of his divine attributes. Because he is just, it follows that injustice will be met with his disfavor. Because he is merciful, mercilessness with be met with his disfavor. Because he is the Ultimate Truth, deception and falsehood are contemptible to him. Simply stated, he hates unjust, unmerciful, deceitful people. This hatred is not an emotional response to their actions; but their actions are antithetical to his divine character. All that God hates resides outside the realm of his favor.

God is love, and his love is available to all receptive hearts. God's love is a sanctuary; it is the secret place of the Most High; a place of favor.

We must however, make a distinction in our thinking between the providential love of God for his creation and his redeeming love for fallen man as proven by the sacrificial death of his son. When God announced the divine edict that the soul that sins will die, it was both an expression of his hatred for sin and his love for mankind. In his foreknowledge, he understood the price that he himself would have to pay for giving man free will. The choice was his alone to make. He consulted with no one. He didn't take a risk, but he did make a perfectly calculated decision, being fully aware that the outcome of his plan would properly secure all of those among the human family that he had chosen. He foreknew and chose all who would respond to his call.

And it is by way of his glorious plan, that he can justly separate the repentant sinner from his sin and see him as covered in righteousness through the righteous shed blood of his son. Glory to his great name!!!

Concerning God, many have not clearly understood that his attributes are fixed, and they are unchangeable. He loves what he loves and hates what he hates, and that can never change. And he could not love any of the children of Adam were it not for his "Covenant Love". This is the love which allowed his beloved son to be tortured on a shameful cross to provide all of humanity a way back from the broken relationship sin caused, to a restored relationship with him.

If we clearly see this, then we know that even those who God calls righteous, have not personally come into God's favor on the merits of their own righteousness, which appears as "filthy rags" in the light of God's pristine holiness. (Isaiah 64:6).

So, in review, the truth is, that a natural man is from birth, spiritually disconnected from God because of sin. All he had to do to become a sinner is to be born. He is born in sin and as his life unfolds, immoral thoughts and behavior begin to find expression in him. He is totally unaware of the invisible influences that are constantly seeking to express themselves through him. He is not in a spiritual battle. He is captured. (2nd Timothy 2:26).

It is impossible for him to know the hidden truths of life apart from a spiritual rebirth. The starting point of this "journey" is at the hearing, believing, and receiving of the good news of the gospel. All who do so can then, begin to re-establish their worldviews, moving them out of darkness into the light of God.

Because the scriptures encourage God's people to establish their worldviews on the sure foundation of his word, and to look ahead thru the eyes of faith to that "perfect day"; or generation.

What we all know about this present natural life; believer and unbeliever alike, is that it is not our permanent state.

Death reigns alongside of life according to this human experience. So then, because we are all mortal; subject to death, all this incomplete and temporary knowledge will someday, vanish. The time is approaching for all of us when all the knowledge of earthly matters we have accumulated over the years will be of no value. I am sure that it has occurred to not all, but many in this world, that life as we know it, will not continue on this planet indefinitely. Make no mistake about this: Life never stops being life, but it absolutely DOES change habitations.

The question is then, what will it all have meant?

Well, the word of God does not simply "drop us off" at the end of this natural life into some inexplicable state of nothingness; but rather, it takes us on a glorious journey down a stream that leads to the "ocean of eternity."

So then, when I say that life, according to the title of this book, is a journey through the mind of God, here is fundamentally what I mean: *Life is the eternal procession of God's thoughts and ideas. Reality is whatever is conceived in His eternal mind. All possibility resides within His infinite and eternal being. Life is the very essence of God.*

Every expression, or "Word" of God is accompanied by divine action, or movement of his Spirit; and every movement of

God is life. No man has seen God (the Creator) at any time. But the Lord God (the Maker) has been seen by certain ones all down through human history. Moses (Exodus 33:20), Jacob (Genesis 32:30) and everyone who saw Jesus Christ when he was on earth, was looking at God. The Son of God in the gospel is the Lord God of Genesis 2. He is the eternal uncreated Word, Expression, Manifestation of the otherwise unknowable God who is omnipresent. This truth is in fact, the only way "personhood" could be correctly ascribed to him.

Saint John 1 1 informs us that the ***Word is inseparably connected to God; for the Word became flesh and dwelt among us. He was named Yahushua; or Jesus. He is the manifestation of God's personhood; the only means by which the infinite invisible God will ever be visibly knowable. He himself informs us that to see him is to see the Father. (John 14:9).***

Fallen man has many theories. Some say: life all began by an accidental explosion that occurred billions of years ago by way of random cosmic activity; in other words, no divine will; just blind luck or chance. Some others who agree, say life is meaningless; that all purpose ends at death. Yet some of the very ones who subscribe to this philosophy are laboring diligently to find ways to perpetuate this so-called "meaningless life" and preserve it for generations to come. Why? It is because whatever perception of life's meaning is embraced by men, life itself, is precious to most. The few fleeting years we live in this natural world, on this convulsing planet are but a blink of the eye in the light of eternity. Time cannot be suspended. It is an unstoppable phenomenon.

Think about this: By the time I finish this sentence, recently published statistics predict that approximately sixteen people will have died in the world. Death has made us to understand the temporary nature of this present life, but is there really nothing else to come afterwards?

One popular worldview is captured in the saying: "Eat, drink, and be merry, for tomorrow we die." The inspiration for such a saying is obviously born out of the anticipation of ensuing death.

Most of us have come to realize that there are continual choices to be made during the living out of our days. What then, are the most important among the many? Which are the most consequential?

We know that it is in the exercise of these choices that we establish our values; determining and manifesting what matters to us; and these values establish our lifestyles. So, here's the question posed to those who do not stand upon the firm foundation of the word of God: "Life": Is there ultimately, an enduring purpose that underlies its existence; or is it in the end, meaningless.

The people who contend that life is meaningless must *illogically dismiss* the idea of an Intelligent Creator and Designer, **for one cannot reasonably acknowledge the existence of a Creator and still hold to the proposition that life has no meaning or purpose.** The irony of their position lies in the fact that <u>they must intentionally disregard undeniable evidence all around them every day, while the God they deny would be pleased to reveal Himself to them if they would earnestly seek Him, or even be amenable to the truth when it appears to them.</u> ***What a rebellious heart doesn't want is the <u>accountability</u> that comes along with the recognition of a God not of its own design.***

But to those of us who believe in the one and only God who is revealed in the Holy Bible, great revelation has come. <u>Jesus said: "I am come that they might have life, and that they may have it more abundantly." (Saint John 10:10) A person can live to be 120 years old and still not have the abundant life that Jesus was speaking of. They may enjoy every single one of all the finer things of this temporary, fading life and still not have it. This abundant life to which Jesus refers is eternal life.</u>

We have come to know that *this temporary journey through this material world is just the beginning; the trial period before the glorious manifestation of the sons of God, who we believers, in fact, are.*

Different people perceive things differently. Natural men operate on differing levels of moral integrity; but the degree of depravity residing in the sinful heart is humanly incomprehensible. No matter what universally applicable societal laws or rules of conduct are established, the sinful human heart is not regulated by them. No written law can for example, transform the heart of a racist. The ability of the human heart to move people down certain paths it has selected is undeniable.

So then, we have understood that good and evil are the constant contestants for the human conscience. The Apostle Paul said in Romans 7 21: "I find then a law, that, when I would do good, evil is present with me." And there is no greater evil to afflict the human family than falsehood; deception, "the lie". For wherever it is permitted to exist, truth has departed. Deception is always working towards bringing man into some type of bondage. Rarely are the deceived familiar with the deceiver for it is obvious that they don't even know that they are deceived. Think about it. If they knew they were being deceived, wouldn't they change their course of action? There is an unseen world of reality all around us that relatively few of us humans are even meaningfully aware. That is why in the discussion of this subject, so many people speak in such vague terms. Some say things like: "I believe there is something out there." What in the world does that mean, other than a confession that they have never bothered to give the matter any serious thought? Some people have succumbed to such gullibility as to accept almost anything at face value.

Many of those who have chosen to deny God's existence would also have us believe concerning life that: "What you see is what you get; and that's all there is." But nothing could be further from the truth! The truth is that all of humanity has been under siege by unseen assailants ever since the first man and woman came to life in this world.

Man does not practice sinful deeds because he was originally designed that way by God! He was originally good; and by the word "good" I don't mean "nice" or "decent". I mean good in the sense of being fully functional according to divine design. That is how the word is used in Genesis to describe the condition of all that God created and made. When a car battery dies, we call it a dead battery. The only hope for it to ever be useful again is if it can be charged. If the cells are dead, the battery is useless. In most cases, people are aware of their action and know when they are doing right or wrong. That's why humans must disregard their inherent sense of right and wrong to do evil. Of course, some people's consciences have been rendered defective and incapable of rightly discerning good from evil because of false indoctrination or willful sinning.

The natural man's spirit is dead to the things of God, and the only way it can be revived is that it must be born again. Otherwise, it is no longer good for the purpose for which it was designed. It is then, like the battery with the dead cells.

The entire planet is saturated with misunderstanding about a multitude of issues. The plain truth is: life has meaning, and actions have consequences.

But the only way the concept of life having no meaning, makes any sense at all, is if, by this concept, it is meant that temporary physical life has no *enduring* meaning or purpose. If death ends all, and the dead have become non-existent, then it would be true that life ultimately, has no meaning or purpose.

But why should even a secular person believe that death ends all, when it is so logically contrary to our experience in life? After all, we live in a natural world of activity rooted in purpose, yet purpose itself, is an unseen reality. Can you put purpose on a scale and weigh it? Of course not, because it is unseen; yet it is real and often "shows up" after it has completed its work. The point is: should we only believe in what we can see, hear, taste, touch, or smell? Of course not, and none of us do.

I have never been able, *with my own two eyes*, to directly observe my own face. In sixty-six years, all I have ever been able to do is see a *reflection* of it by a mirror, or some other secondary source. I have seen the effects of air, but air itself, I have never seen. Yet, I fully believe in the existence of this life-sustaining element. Don't you?

Everything within us that empowers us to think, choose, and act is intangible and unseen. We experience reality in every moment of our lives without <u>ever </u>having physically seen it. What all of us physically see are merely symbols, or representations of <u>unseen reality.</u> Only the "truly blind" deny that this temporary life is *filled* with meaning and purpose. And it is vitally important for us to know that *there are critical choices to be made during this interval between birth and death. There is reality and there is unreality, and it is vitally important that we, during our brief stay here in life, come to the truth.*

When we look at ourselves in the mirror and come to realize that what we see is merely the "physical house" we live in, is it not wise then, for us to think more deeply about what really constitutes life?

I am convinced that most humans instinctively sense that life is more than a meaningless game of chance culminating at death to some vanishing point void of all purpose. It's just that humanly speaking; most folks don't clearly know what to make of it. Man's fears, delights, hopes, dreams, and aspirations are <u>all</u> shaped by his beliefs about life; and <u>what we believe in our hearts is said to be for each of us, "our reality"</u> so long as we adhere to such beliefs.

But what we vitally need to understand is that *"our reality" is not necessarily......reality!* You know why? Because **what we believe may or may not be true. Our beliefs change, but reality cannot change.** It is eternally established by God. Times and circumstances change but reality does not.

What we believe today may change tomorrow, but reality remains the same. It was whatever it was yesterday, and it is what it is today. And if what we believe is true, it is also real; but if what we believe is untrue, it is also unreal. I may be fully convinced that I, through the "power of positive thinking," can fly, but if, based upon this belief, I should leap from a twenty-story building to soar the heavens, I will instead, plunge to the earth and die! My positive thinking will not re-direct the law of gravity. Only a word from God calling for such a miracle can do that, in which case I would soar like an eagle! Just because brain activity is going on in your head, it cannot automatically be assumed that the thoughts you entertain are in flow with what is true. Nothing we think, will, desire, believe, or choose *creates* reality; not even if we receive the thing we hoped and believed for.

Unreality may be defined as any phenomena that God allows to exist apart from his perfect will. That is why unbelievers often prosper in this material world in many cases far beyond the material prosperity of believers. There are universal laws of prosperity that will be effective if applied by believer and unbeliever alike. Sinful man can gain the temporary world, while losing his soul. So says our Lord in Mark 8:36. In this case, prosperity has failed to awaken his spiritual mind. He is wealthy, but his soul continues to reside in the realm of unreality.

Please understand that as the people of God, we are not able to create reality, but we <u>are:</u> able to *connect* with it through faith, which is for the believer, "the substance of things hoped for and the evidence of things not seen." (Hebrews 11:1)

Many Christians are confused about this verse of scripture and think that they can "use their faith" as the substance; or raw material out of which *they* can produce the things they hope for. There is power in positive thinking when your positive thoughts and speech are according to the truth. But they did not "create" that truth; they simply "connected" with it. In every case, the effect of that connection come from the divine source. The misunderstanding lies in who it is that uses our faith. When fallen man places his faith in something real and gets results he attributes his success to things that don't honor God.

But it is <u>God</u> who <u>uses</u> our faith as "substance "or; "raw material"; not us. If faith is only substance; or "raw material

", who turns it into the finished product; us? I think not. If we could do it ourselves, why ask God? Our job is to present our unwavering faith to Him. But we, as believers must believe and confess what is true. God will never answer prayers that are contrary to his will and character no matter how much faith you have in such prayers.

Reality is not required to change to fit anyone's unwavering faith, but it already fit's unwavering faith in that which is grounded in truth. Reality fits truth and truth fits reality. If we believe with all our hearts that God is, our unwavering faith is not what makes it so. It is because *God is,* that we can believe it to be so. Man's faith did not produce God; nor does his unbelief diminish Him.

Now if those who deny to themselves the existence of an all-knowing, purposeful Creator were right, then it would be true that ultimately, nothing really matters; but because they are wrong, then their "reality" is in fact, unreality.

Since the dawn of human history, there has been an impenetrable wall of separation between those to whom reality has been revealed and to whom it has not. In the Bible, the two groups are identified as "children of light" (regenerated; or "born-again people, and "children of darkness (natural, or "unregenerate people." Reality is not universally evolving over time, but rather, manifesting more and more to the children of light; and becoming more and more indiscernible to the children of darkness. The existence of unseen intelligent evil entities committed to keeping humanity in moral & spiritual darkness is patently real. It is a fact that a vast network of fallen angels and disembodied spirits from another age are among us. They are in fact, wreaking havoc among the human family even as recently as your last exhale. Those who call this statement fiction, are the spiritually dead who are blind to spiritual reality, confined to the world of matter. These are the children of the moral and spiritual darkness of this realm of consciousness.

In a global society shaped by the influences of these unseen evil personalities and the collective power of dominating human will and choice, the "spiritually dead" have developed prevailing world views and socially accepted values that conflict with truth and are thus, in conflict with reality. Therefore, in the Bible, Satan is called" the god of this world (or "age")

All reality is conceived in the mind of God. *Before; during, and after time; reality is! It is not evolving; it is always present tense. Whatever shall be..................is! If God conceived it, it is reality.*

In Malachi 3 6, God says: "I Am Yahweh (THE LORD) I change not...."

We do not all each create our own individual realities by what we accept to be true. Such an idea is absurd. There is **truth and there is untruth**. There is **reality** and there is **unreality**. If we accept to be true, that which is true, we connect to reality. If we accept that which is untrue to be true, we connect to unreality.

There are foundational truths that form the framework of life's true meaning.

79

Ultimate Truth will never be arrived at through the endless pursuits of scientific investigation. While it cannot be denied that scientific research has brought us much important and useful revelation about the nature and laws of life in the material universe, much mystery remains. With each discovery come more unanswered questions. This is because natural man is virtually oblivious to the spiritual reality that he blindly wanders thru. And even the questions concerning this natural life continue to greatly outnumber the answers.

The same experience has occurred in man's pursuit of understanding in every area of life. He can see only the natural. Nor is the spiritual man's understanding of spiritual reality complete or absolute. This simply proves to us all, that man's understanding of any truth is at best, gradual, progressive and limited.

But the spiritual man has access to the things of God by the indwelling of God's Spirit within him. No such access is granted to unbelievers.

So far, many fundamental propositions of science have been successfully tested and proven, and have endured the test of consistency over time, and are in that light, deemed as foundational. Trouble is, many other unsubstantiated theories have been awarded that same status and offered universally to the human family with very little opposition. Largely among the masses, neither the scientific language nor its conclusions are clearly comprehended. Therefore, as ordinary people look to the scholars of science to provide answers to the mysteries of life, the clear majority of them have chosen to place their faith in their findings without questioning the veracity of them. Many fail to see the self-limiting nature of secular scientific investigation which surely will never uncover the mysteries of a reality it deems non-existent.

I join with many others in expressing appreciation for those who have dedicated their lives to the seeking of solutions to problems we face on this journey of life. But there is more to life and reality than that for which our scientific representatives are qualified to provide answers or explanations.

As for morality in our world today, many of its long-believed scripture-based principles have been challenged; and in many cases, completely overturned due to the widespread popularity of immoral practices and the promotion of the worldviews of morally-depraved men. Alternative lifestyles before considered abominable, are now offered to be freely embraced by all consenting adults although God has not endorsed such alternatives. As the days of moral darkness continue, the darkness grows thicker as the lines separating right and wrong become more and more obscured. Evil unseen forces have intensified their efforts because they know their time is almost up. (Revelations 12:12) Good and evil are not eternally coupled together. There is coming, a day when evil shall be no more. Man's unbelief cannot cancel God's purpose.

There has seemingly emerged a "New Morality". But is it new, or is it the old immorality with a "new" name? "As it was in the days of Noah……" (Matthew 24:37). Everything that goes around, comes around.

Faith is a law of life in a world filled with mystery. Pursuit of understanding is good and noble. But misplaced faith in human theory that does not consider undeniable human fallibility is filled with danger.

When our worldviews are exclusively shaped by scientific theory, then the "theories of science" have become for many, the means of access to Ultimate truth. The conclusion that must be ultimately arrived at according to this expression of faith is that "man himself" is the ultimate source of knowledge, wisdom and understanding.

Now then, in the light of these considerations, have we *really* arrived at a point in the unfolding generations of collective human thought where there is no need for people of faith to continue to believe in an *Unseen Supreme Being as revealed in the sacred scriptures*? Perhaps based upon the "encouragement" of the atheists of science, we should simply "dismiss" Him altogether and pay homage to the "god" of "science?"

<u>Let the people of faith cry: "never, never, never"!! May the very idea be cursed at the root!</u>

How many countless lives will continue to be lost or destroyed as ships dashed against the rocks by the pagan god of "science" falsely so-called?

I believe I have been clear on this point, but let me reiterate:

True science is no enemy to the truth because true science <u>is true.</u>

But natural science is no substitute for divine revelation. The full scope of our existence far exceeds the matters about which we humanly concern ourselves in this present state. We are not the central theme of the full measure of this reality we are experiencing called "life." And when we depart from this life, the story of us is not over. The end of this natural life marks the beginning of a new and eternal state of existence. In Revelations 22:11, it seems that human beings are then, at the place of being fixed in either a state of spiritual life or death. The following verses (12-21) serve as an epilogue to end the book with both invitation and warning.

Those who trust themselves fully to the provision and care of the false god of science will discover many facts but will never arrive at the truth. I am not calling science false, but when it is elevated to the place in one's heart that is divinely-designed to be reserved for the Creator, it has become a false god.

Look! There is something radically wrong with man and science can't fix it!

As scientists examine the things that make up the material world, they acknowledge that matter itself, is filled with life, but *life is more than matter; beyond tangibility*, and this book vigorously asserts that the questions pertaining to its meaning extend beyond anything that will be arrived at through the scientific process.

The wind blows. Grass grows. Rocks tumble; but they do so being void of any recognizable processes of thought, desire, or choice. Yet the existence of these and all of life's natural processes express purpose;

But what and who's purpose? Life has an Author. It is certain that the Author of life is not mortal. We mortal creatures participate, but we surely did not originate; nor can we sustain this mystery called "life."

And while there are many "experts" in various fields of study related to this question, in each of them there remains multitudes of unanswered; indeed, seemingly unanswerable questions.

It is because life's reality transcends the realm within which all their investigative boundaries are set. One may as well attempt to tell the <u>exact</u> number of atoms that make up the universe as to give an exact and exhaustive definition of the meaning of life.

The complexities of life are endless. We may acknowledge every human discovery, yet the mysteries that remain before us are infinite.

In addition to the cold emotionless logic of strict science, human life in this world is laughter and tears; successes and failures; pain and pleasure; and infinitely more. These things we humanly identify with through the experience of living; and even in these things, there are so many questions. The greatest mystery in life is life itself. But the answer to the question of life's <u>fundamental</u> meaning and purpose can be known by those of us who trust in the word of God as found in the sacred scriptures. The question of life's ultimate purpose is a question that should be seriously asked; and the answer seriously pursued.

And germane to the success of our arriving at the truth;
or right conclusions is the right method of pursuit.
God's word reveals the truth of what we can know
about life. So then, it will be according to that source
we will seek to find the truth. There is Reality and
there is Unreality. God's word separates the two.
Amen.

CHAPTER 5

"Let Us Make Man"

And God said; "Let us make man in our own image and after our own likeness" …

(Genesis 1 26)

In the beginning, God took from the "dust of the ground" and formed the body of Adam. He then "breathed" into that body the "breath of life." (or "lives") It is at this point that Adam is said to have become a living soul.

Today, a soul comes into existence by natural birth; or reproduction of the original, and ever-existing spirit; or life principle that is inside sperm & egg cells, and this developing soul is endowed with the seeds of all human attributes. Indeed, the same "breath of life" God breathed into Adam, is still reproducing human beings; or souls today. Biblically, we are called "souls", and each of us are living beings through the reproduction of the original divine union of body and spirit.

And remember; a soul is made up of the unseen attributes of mind, will, and emotion. We are made in the image and after the likeness of God because ***essentially, each of us is an "unseen reality" .... JUST LIKE GOD!***

We cannot tell with certainty how long a time passed between the creating of Adam and the making of Eve, because the idea of God's creative morning and evening should not be understood as a 24-hour solar day. The scriptures inform us that God put the man to sleep and took a rib from his side and formed the woman; or "man with a womb." Both of them were formed on the same creative day, the duration of which has been revealed to no one. Jesus told us that these things are not for us to know. (Acts 1:7). But of course, the duration of a solar day is common knowledge, because this information was developed, and authorized by man to serve man. But it should be clear, that the handiwork of God cannot be confined within such parameters. There is so much to discuss about this entire narrative of human creation that must be kept for a later time in another chapter, in perhaps, even another book.

Adam was a "son of God"

When God formed Adam from the dust of the ground and breathed spirit into him, his soul was awakened, and he became a son of God. Adam was never a baby, but he was a man-child.

It is believed that he was created with the ability to commune with his Father, God, intuitively as well as through the processes of language and speech.

Today, modern man should perhaps think of Adam as a sort of "template" for all that a natural man would become. After all; he was the first to discover and utilize all the abilities innate in humanity.

This, he was privileged to do through the direct nurture and developmental guidance of his father, God.

It is unknown how long Adam lived before God performed the divine operation on him that produced the first woman, Eve.

The two of them were the first fully-developed human beings on the day of their births.

We don't know whether Adam was only a few days older than Eve, or a few weeks, months, or years.

How long a time did Father God spend with Adam educating him about the nature of the world in which he had been placed before Eve came on the scene?

How much did God show him? We have no certain answers for such questions. It is important here, that we have clear and scriptural understanding of the Biblical uses of the term: "son, or sons of God."

We will consider throughout this writing, the usage of the term in four distinct references:

1. As it refers to angels. (Genesis 6 2, Job 2 1)
2. As it refers to Adam (Luke 3 38)

3.   As it refers to Jesus Christ (John 1 14)
4.   As it refers to born-again believers (1ˢᵗ John 3 2)

Adam was not the first of the sons of God

<u>Angels</u>

In God's divine interrogation of Job in Chapter 37, He asks in verse 7 at the completion of the formation of the earth, where was he (verse 4) during the great celestial celebration "When the morning stars sang together, and all the sons of God shouted for joy?"

This verse informs us that these angels called sons of God had already been created before the original creation of the earth.

God is Spirit and angels are spirits. (Hebrews 1 7) They are servant; or ministering spirits (14).

They are distinct individual intelligent personalities endowed with powers and abilities that surpass those possessed by human beings. But man is said to be only a "little lower" than the angels because he is mortal. Angels are not subject to death.

So then, before Adam, God created celestial beings that He called "sons" whom we have come to know as angels. These supernatural sons of God are distinguished from Adam primarily by their immortality. They also, not having been created for reproduction, are genderless.

By this fact, we do not say that they are incapable of reproductive powers, for the range of their abilities has not been conclusively disclosed to us. But according to what has been revealed in scripture, such activity is contrary to their divine purpose seeing they are immortal.

<u>Adam</u>

Luke 8 38 calls Adam the son of God. It could be no other way, for he was, in this dispensation, the first of his kind. He was the direct workmanship of God; formed by God's own "supernatural hand." The same life-giving spirit that had brought the angels into being had now been "breathed" by God Himself into Adam.

This man of clay was a spirit-being indwelling a material body, and as such, was related to both the realm of the invisible spiritual world and the visible, natural world. This distinguishes Adam as a different kind of son than the angels.

According to the Genesis account, the first human family on earth knew the one and only God. The generations immediately following also knew Him. But as the generations progressed, the knowledge of God was not retained and passed on.

Mankind began to push the thoughts of God and their accountability to Him away from themselves. Their lust for independence moved them to destroy the voice of conscience by indulging in those practices condemned by it. The consequent response from God was that He, in turn, released them to pursue their lusts.

The voice of conscience, through which He communicated with them, became progressively fainter.

The unseen supernatural restraints God had set to protect them from themselves, and invisible assailants were lifted.

The truths about God were forgotten. The ensuing generations came to know nothing of Him, as the whole human race continued to plummet to unprecedented depths of moral decadence. (Read Romans 1 18 thru 32)

Because divine judgment was not swiftly executed against rebellious humanity, men were emboldened to pursue their wickedness with reckless abandon. They did not hesitate to pursue every evil pleasure they conceived in their hearts.

The hearts of men became increasingly corrupt, producing extreme violence, perversions of every sort, liars and deceivers, mockers and haters of all that is good, right and true; unclean and impure men, women and children. Yet the consciences continued to speak; if only now in a faint whisper… "God is." So, to finally put an end to this faint but annoying voice of conviction, many of them began to conceive gods to their own liking. According to today's language, you might call them "user-friendly gods."

Others set themselves up as religious leaders teaching demonically-inspired false doctrine claiming to show others the way to "god", and by so doing, gained power to exploit and control them.

At that point, the lying spirits that had provided them with false inspiration achieved their objective: the deadening of the convicting voice of conscience. The original voice of a good conscience in them was now completely displaced, and in its stead, the voice of an evil conscience would speak. ***Now they could*** <u>*continue in their evil deeds*</u> ***and*** <u>*practice religion at the same time*</u>. Yet even in its severely weakened state, the voice of conscience would continue to speak; no longer to convict or convince but to condemn!

The reprobate could enjoy their indulgences in sinful pleasure, but their souls would never know peace. ("There is no peace, saith my God, to the wicked."- Isaiah 57 21) They did not understand that it is a dangerous thing to take the name of the Lord in vain.

Those who *speak* the truths of God out of their mouths, while *rejecting* them in practice, purporting themselves to be His spokesmen, are <u>hypocrites</u> and <u>false messengers.</u>

It is a dangerous thing to call upon the name of the Lord while there is no intention in one's rebellious heart to repent. *To add religion to rebellion* will produce <u>demonic control over one's life.</u> This is presumptuous sinning. The presumptuous sinner may call upon the name of the Lord all he wants but the Lord will not respond. (Psalms 66 18) This does not mean that he will not get a "deceitful word"; receive a "false vision" or experience

a "fake miracle." But it <u>does</u> mean that the word, vision, or miracle will not be from God!

2nd Corinthians 11 14 says that: "Satan himself is transformed into an angel of light."

<u>Those who do not love the **truth** will fall victim to the **lie.**</u>

It is interesting to note that according to Genesis 4 26, <u>during the generation of Enos, "men began to call upon the name of the Lord</u>." This could lead us to believe that a revival had begun in that ancient world, but curiously, nothing else is said about the matter. This is because there had been no revival or restoration to godly reverence taking place. Instead, it was a demonically-inspired revolution of false religion. <u>The people began to use the NAME OF THE LORD in vain, attaching it to perverse practices to embellish them with a deceptive appearance of sacredness.</u> Much of this goes on today in Christendom. This is witchcraft, and through these practices, they opened spiritual doors for hordes of evil angelic spirits to invade the earth resulting in the divine judgment of the flood of Noah's day.

God continues in this mode of operation to this very day. When men are willfully ignorant of truth available to them because they have no desire for it, God fixes the eyes that <u>will not see</u> so that they <u>cannot see!</u>

The same God who gives more grace to the humble of heart will harden those who harden their own hearts against the truth. (Romans 9 18) All of them who did not desire the truth and turned away from it were left by God to their own devices. God would allow deception to overtake them, for they had no taste for the truth. Disobedience had "spawned many children." (Ephesians 2 2)

From the days of Cain and those days that would follow, even until this very day, a false god rules in the hearts of the children of disobedience; to whom all of us have at one time, been subject.

They were and are counted as reprobates whose minds are no longer capable of perceiving spiritual truth; "children of the lie;" adopted into the "Satanic family." (Saint John 8 40 thru 47)

Yet sinful men are still quite capable of believing in the existence of God. God continues to search people's hearts; not looking for some sort of tainted self-produced goodness within their fallen sinful natures, but for a willingness to believe…that God is!

What then, is a reprobate mind? It is a mind that is no longer rightly influenced by the voice of conscience. It is a mind under the dominion of sinful lusts; evil imaginations; and idolatrous self-love. All these things serve to severely distort one's perception of truth.

In the case of reprobates, pure reason is heavily clouded by damaged; or distorted emotions, producing wrong; often tragically wrong choices. Clearly, a reprobate mind is a mind under satanic control. Is a reprobate mind unsavable? yes, because it will never submit to the will of God on its own. And God will not bring the rebellious along with the obedient to heaven.

But Jesus came to destroy the works of the devil. That is why I said before that a man may seek after God and find Him, but only because God; the searcher of hearts has first sought after the man.

But according to divine mercy, there has always been an unseen supernatural restraint in the earth realm due to the presence of the Holy Spirit. This is the longsuffering of God Himself. (Read Genesis 6 3; 2nd Thessalonians 2 1 thru 7; 2nd Peter 3 8 & 9) Because God is not willing that any should perish, He raises up intercessors to cry unto Him in behalf of a perishing world so that He might thereby extend His mercy.

Were this not so, fallen man would have long ago, been totally overwhelmed by satanic and demonic influences, thereby having no access to God.

If God would have ever given Satan free, and uninhibited reign over humanity, all the atrocities of human history would have seemed as mere child's play compared to what the devil would have already done.

Man's survival on this planet is not <u>because</u> of himself; it is <u>despite</u> himself! World wars are a testament to man's self-destructive nature. Man was not designed by God to direct his own steps (Jeremiah 10 23) None of us knows the extreme depths of wickedness as does Satan, for it is His constant meditation, having in fact, become the embodiment of it.

His absolute hatred of humanity is hidden under the "cloak of deception."

Given his full way, he would have perhaps, led man to annihilate himself long ago. That is of course, unless man's prolonged suffering (which perhaps is surely the case) would heighten the gratification of his evil desires.

Job's wife, overwhelmed by the suffering she watched her husband endure, advised him to "curse God and die!" (Job 2 9) I am convinced that the suffering she witnessed her husband endure was incomprehensible and more than her mind could bear. It seems that to her, nothing was worth the kind of torment she was watching him endure.

Job had been married to this woman for several years. Surely, he knew her more intimately than perhaps anyone on earth. Although he did say that according to what I believe was her emotionally-born advice; that she <u>spoke</u> as one of the foolish women, he <u>never </u>directly called her a foolish woman. I suspect that she was not simply a "foolish woman." Undoubtedly, few of those women by whom she would be so identified, had witnessed anything in their lives to be compared with Mrs. Job's experience.

Now isn't it powerfully interesting that God rebuked the three friends of Job for misrepresenting Him (Job 42 7 thru 9) and never uttered a word of rebuke against Job's wife who advised him to "curse God and die."? God did not judge and destroy her; nor did He provide Job with another wife. It was she who bore Job the seven sons and three daughters that God would bless Job with after the loss of his first children… The fact that this woman's womb was still fruitful was itself, a mark of divine favor.

But Job, a godly man greatly tested, but not beyond what he could bear (1st Corinthians 10:13), maintained his integrity, thereby providing a "covering" for his wife; his helper; his soul-mate; his "weaker vessel." (1st Peter 3:7) For God made the man to be the head of the woman (1st Corinthians 11 3) and made him responsible to provide a spiritual covering; or protection for her because of the (wicked) angels (or seducing spirits) (1st Corinthians 11: 9 & 10) who would deceive her by way of her natural femininity.

In contrast, I believe that Adam failed his wife Eve in this respect. The command was directly given to Adam not to eat of the tree of the knowledge of good and evil. At that time, as I said earlier, Eve had not even been made yet!

So then, according to all that scripture reveals, Eve only received the command concerning God's prohibition second handedly. The Tempter came and beguiled Eve in the very presence of Adam, and Adam "spoke not a mumbling word!" He simply joined Eve in partaking of the forbidden fruit. (Genesis 3:1thru 6)

Now at the beginning, Adam seemed to be aware of his headship, speaking God-endorsed, authoritative and enduring words over his helpmate. He named her "Ishshah"; or "Woman."

He realized that she was a part of him, for she had been taken out of Him. He also decreed that the bond between them should never be broken, but the two of them should be one flesh. (Genesis 2 21 thru 24) Perhaps it was this very decree that led him to submit to his wife's error rather than to bring correction, and thereby covering.

From the moment the deceived woman acted independently of her husband, drawing him through his own weakness, into disobedience, observe the nature of Eve's speech thereafter.

But first consider that by this time, nothing much else is ever said about Adam other than that he "knew"; or made love to his wife.

By then, he seemed to be merely, an absentee; or at least indifferent father and husband who only showed up to "know" his wife. The last thing recorded to have been spoken by Adam in the narrative is that he called his wife's name "Eve."

(Genesis 3:20)

From then on, we hear exclusively, from Eve.

When Cain was born, she said "I," not "we," have gotten a man; or male child from the Lord. (Genesis 4:1) After Cain slew Abel, at some point, Adam successfully impregnates his wife again.

Again, there is no word from Adam, but Eve discerns and declares: "The Lord has appointed me; not "us" another seed instead of Abel whom Cain slew." (4:25)

Surely there should not be more read into this than the simple reading and considering of what the narrative seems to infer, but one thing is for sure: accountability for the keeping of God's command rested firstly, upon the shoulders of Adam; not Eve.

It is also clearly revealed as we continue, that jealousy, hatred and violence established their roots within the <u>very first family</u>; for within it, the first murder occurs. Thousands of years later, man in all his "wisdom" has found no solution to his moral depravity. Can he survive; or will he ultimately destroy himself? If so, in that case what then, was the purpose of his life?

CHAPTER 6

The Spellbinder and the Spell-breaker

"The thief does not come except to steal, and to kill, and to destroy. I have come that they may have life, and that they may have it more abundantly. (John 10:10 -NKJV)

Those of us who believe in the divine inspiration of scripture, believe wholeheartedly in the reality of the unseen. God has allowed some of us a glimpse into that which is beyond the temporal; the material realm.

Many other believers have not become seekers. These have seemingly been content with being delivered from the lost condition they were in, and have settled right there, because they are not pilgrims; they are settlers. They "go to Church" on Sunday and............ well; actually, that's it. They are not followers; they are settlers. But Jesus did not call us to be settlers. In the NLT translation, Matthew 16:24, Jesus said: "If any of you wants to be my follower, you must turn from your selfish ways, take up your cross, and follow me".

The settler is too much at home in this perishing world social system. He or she has either forgotten, or never known that the child of God's citizenship is in heaven. – Philippians 3:20. They are so deeply involved in the world's affairs that they can no longer be distinguished from the world.

Let me be candid here. To be a settler instead of a follower will stagnate your faith. And stagnant faith has ceased to be in motion, making it a stationary target for the fiery darts of the enemy. And the enemy has many fiery darts aimed at our hearts.

How can a child of God be comfortable while settled in enemy territory? And by enemy territory, please understand that I am not referring to the natural world; planet earth. We are not aliens. This planet is clearly our present residence, but we are already, while here on earth, eternal citizens of heaven. That is why we must not allow our temporary residence here to become a sidetrack; a reroute onto a false lifestyle that is distant from the way of the Lord.

To examine ourselves to see if we have become settlers, we may candidly ask ourselves, "How comfortable are we in the company of them who practice sinful behavior? Is fellowship with them something you engage in of necessity for love of their souls, and for opportunity to share Christ with them? If so, please know that you cannot win them for Jesus while doing what they do. If your lifestyle demonstrates very little difference from theirs, you have become a settler. You are a worldly believer.

The world is the world…and the Church is the Church!

Consider the story of Abraham's nephew, Lot, a man that Peter called righteous (2nd Peter 2:8) who took his family and settled in the wicked city of Sodom. Peter said that Lot's righteous soul was tormented day after day as he and his family were exposed to the chaotic, lawless, and rampant lascivious activity that saturated that city.

But what would a righteous man find appealing about such a godless place as Sodom? He clearly did not choose to follow the example of his uncle Abraham, a godly man and a sojourner who chose a nomadic lifestyle over an environment void of God. But instead, he allowed himself to become established in a corrupt society whose vile conduct left him in mental and emotional anguish every day.

It is an undeniable fact that settling and remaining in an environment of people practicing perverse living is dangerous because "Evil communication corrupts good manners." (1st Corinthians 15:33) The children of God must always remember to bear in mind that we are in the world but not of the world.

Living too close to the world will so dull the believer's spiritual senses that the lines between purity and impurity will become obscure. Moral principles will be compromised. It is as impossible for a child of God who is walking with Jesus to live in fellowship with ungodly people as it is for the blending of light and darkness. The two are eternally opposed to one another. Attempts at blending the two is an exercise in futility. Even as there can be no successful mixing of oil with water, you simply cannot harmoniously mix flesh and spirit. Jesus said in Saint John 3:6, "That which is born of the flesh is flesh; and that which is born of the Spirit is spirit."

This proves for us that there is no such thing as the union of flesh and spirit. And since the children of God live by the Spirit, we should also walk by; or practice a lifestyle that is in harmony with the Spirit. Neither the carnal believer nor the unregenerate man are in flow with the Holy Spirit, but only the carnal man is out of place. The unregenerate man lives in the darkness. He is at home there, and will remain in that state until he comes to God in repentance by receiving the gospel of salvation. But the carnal believer is a child of light wandering around in the darkness.

Please understand, children of God: We are not the light; but we have been delivered out of the darkness to bear witness of the Light (John 1:8) just like John the Baptist.

In the case of Lot, it's clear that there was in he and his family, a good measure of attachment to, and acceptance of this corrupt community. Lot was grieved by the evil he exposed himself and his family to, but he did nothing about it. He compromised his morals and exposed himself and his entire family to the influence of evil spirits. How distorted was his judgement that he would offer his two virgin daughters to a mob of homosexual men? How distorted had his reasoning processes become? They had no interest in his daughters. They were banging on his door demanding that he release the two "men" they saw enter his home. I wonder what thoughts the daughters had about their father after this incident?

Apparently, his wife was so emotionally attached to this place that even while escaping for her life, her heart was still longing for that place. Sodom seems to have not only become an acceptable place for her, but had grown in her heart to become a treasure. In Matthew 6:21, Jesus said: "For where your treasure is, there will your heart be also."

The atmosphere of this entire world is filled with evil unseen influences that have captivated the minds of the multitudes that inhabit this world. Only those of us who by grace, are known of God, have been delivered from the spiritual darkness that engulfs the world and blinds the minds of the ungodly. But there is yet much to know about how to live to stay free.

What? Did you think that because you are a believer and were set free, you were "home free"?

Let's be clear. The moment God saved you, you became another member of Satan's special "hit list."

The natural residents of this fallen world are under his spell; under the influence of a compelling speaker of lies who has captivated multitudes of both human and angelic beings. He will be identified here as the Spellbinder; also known scripturally as the father of lies. He is the original rebel; the first created being known in scripture to oppose God. I call him the spellbinder because in 1st Samuel 15:23, we are informed that rebellion is as the sin of witchcraft. Witchcraft involves the casting of spells and the invocation of evil spirits. This rebel has a host of angels and evil spirits at his command who are dispatched throughout the earth.

Okay. What exactly is a spell? Well, it is a psychological, emotional condition that holds a person in a certain state of mind. Satan, the spellbinder is an unseen enemy who is at his best when he is successful at drawing man's attention away from the right thoughts. He lures man away from right thoughts to wrong thoughts that appear to be right. Once the mind is led astray, he continues to lure you further and further from the right path until he has you completely out of touch with the truth and fully embracing a lie.

Sometimes, people deceive their own selves by developing new perspectives about matters that were at one time, settled. Their perspective changed because their feelings changed.

Sometimes, people reject what they know to be good simply because they have no taste for it. They deny this as the reason for their having turned from the good, and act as though they had no other choice but to accept the lesser of two evils. What they once correctly considered wrong gradually morphed into something acceptable. But many times, it is simply Satanic enticements that have attached themselves to the sinful lusts of man's fallen human nature. In such cases, the man has lost the ability to see the truth because he has turned from it and taken the bait fed to him by the Spellbinder. The vocabulary of Satan is the great poison of the world.

From the earliest days of human history, the tool of deceitful words has been employed by him to allure man away from the light into the shadowy regions of darkness.

It's clear that this great deceiver has a burning hatred for humanity. HE IS THE UNSEEN MASTER MANIPULATOR BEHIND THE HUMAN MANIPULATORS OF THIS WORLD. All underhanded, calculating, conniving people are themselves victims of this master manipulator, and have unwittingly surrendered their consciences to be seared. A seared conscience is clearly defective and untrustworthy to make proper moral judgements.

One common characteristic of all manipulators, spirit or human: They study their victims to detect their areas of weakness and exploit them by using those weaknesses against them. This, in fact, is our adversary's unrelenting campaign strategy against the entire human family. There is nothing he hates more than innocence. He chafes at the thought of there being any soul that he cannot effectively accuse before God. He hates grace.

The Spellbinder's greatest accomplice is sin; sin at work in the human nature. His angels seek opportunities to present sinful things to you that your flesh already finds desirable. They pay attention to what your eyes are drawn to. If we humans can understand body language, do you think that evil spirits who have been studying humans since the beginning cannot? They watch when you swell with pride or exaggerate a story to impress others. They see when you use manipulation to get others to do your bidding.

He asked Eve: Is that what God told you; that if you eat fruit from this tree that you would surely die? Nah; Eve. You won't surely die! He just doesn't want you to see things clearly. He's trying to keep you from reaching your potential. If you eat this fruit, you'll be a lot like him. Then you can be independent of him and you'll know for yourself what's good and what's not. (My paraphrase here)

I'm sure you can see that the central theme of his discourse with Eve was designed to birth a false impression in her mind about God. Very pointedly, he urged Eve to defy God's words, that they were not true, and that God had an ulterior motive. He alleged that God didn't want them to discover their own "godhood," so that they could be independent. Inferentially speaking, he was saying to Eve, "You guys could be doing your own thing around here without having to always be checking in with God." "After all, once you have a bite of that delicious fruit, you will be free of this innocent naiveté and you will know good and evil by personal experience. I promise: you and Adam will never be the same.

Now we know that Satan's dialogue with Eve was designed to use a true statement infused with the lying suggestion that this would simply be a good thing; no worries, right? Wrong. He told her that their eyes would be opened, and their eyes were opened. But they had elected to disobey God. And they would soon thereafter, discover that they had been awakened to a new level of awareness that also introduced them to feelings that they had never experienced before; guilt, shame, fear, sorrow, anger, jealousy, and many more emotions which they would quickly experience.

And one thing was for certain. Innocence was lost. The awakening of the conscience was necessary for these free-willed human creatures who had breached God's command. They would develop to learn imperfectly, through the experience of living, what is good and what is evil. God chose to expose them to the possibility; even the susceptibility of failure. He said to us all, through the prophet: "See, I have set before thee this day, life and good, and death and evil." – Deuteronomy 30:15. He desires for us to freely and willingly serve him. Those who think they are living independent of him are clinging to a spiritual illusion.

People who try to live life without recognition of God fail to realize that they are nonetheless subject to him; even in their rebellion. They fail to realize that there is a foreordained destiny for the rebellious as well as the obedient. The fate of both the obedient and the disobedient are in their own hands, but the outcome of all choices is predetermined by God alone.

Now Adam and Eve had also learned something else about this matter of good and evil. They came to realize that within their own minds these two concepts seemed to be opposing one another. But prior to their disobedience, they had never had an evil thought. Before eating the forbidden fruit, there was no way for them to consciously sin; in fact, the idea of sinning had never even occurred to them until the serpent planted the thought in their minds. They became sin-conscious when their "eyes were opened" and consciences, awakened.

I don't know if they understood the principle of sin as such. This seems doubtful to me. But if Adam and Eve retained the memories of life in the garden before their disobedience, their memories had to present to them a stark contrast to their state of life after the fall.

God pronounced sentence on all parties. The man and woman were banished from the garden. Satan had finished using the reptile who goes upon his belly and slithers away as Satan departs from it. As far as we can tell by the scriptures, neither Adam nor Eve were ever aware of the adversary; that old serpent; the devil, who was indwelling the snake. In fact, revelation about Satan's existence didn't become common until New Testament times.

It is important to note that Adam, the original man out of whom Eve, the original woman was taken was divinely designated to rule on earth with the assistance of his God-given life partner. Concerning the tree of life, it is clear from Genesis 2:16 that the command not to eat of that forbidden tree was specifically to Adam. Eve had not even been designed and taken from Adam's side. Nor do the scriptures say that God gave separate instructions to Eve concerning this matter.

If this is the case, we understand why Eve was not charged with the transgression.

The first mention of sin in the Bible is in Genesis 4:6 & 7 (NLT). In those verses, God says to Cain: "Why are you so angry? Why do you look so dejected?" You will be accepted if you do what is right. But if you refuse to do what is right, then watch out! Sin is crouching at the door, eager to control you. But you must subdue it and be its master." But Cain did not rule over those angry, hateful thoughts by repenting and humbling himself before God. Nor did he make a single attempt to go back and do it right by presenting the acceptable sacrifice. Instead, he chose to demonstrate contempt for God's extension of grace, and in so doing, gave himself over to the wicked one. (1ˢᵗ John 3:12). He allowed his heart to entertain murderous thoughts about his brother, and went on to murder him. The heart of Cain was fertile soil for the evil seed of the enemy.

You see, Lucifer, the anointed Cherub had been demoted and become the devil, banished with all his hoard of angelic defectors from heaven prior to the failure of Cain. Exactly how long ago this angelic rebellion occurred, or when they took up residence in the atmosphere, on, around and under the earth is unknown. But his tactics have not changed. He is still covertly alluring souls towards evil pleasures while sin lies in wait at the doorway of man's heart.

The Spellbinder wants to make you your own worst enemy. And he's thrilled to know that you don't believe he is real because he runs a covert operation. Both carnal believers and unbelievers will continue to wrestle with flesh and blood and never realize that doing this is about as futile as a person trying to outbox his own shadow. One can never outbox his own shadow.

Well, if what we have discussed in this chapter thus far was the whole story, then mankind would be left languishing in a world of moral and spiritual darkness without hope. But thanks be to our Champion; our Mighty Lord and Savior, Jesus Christ, God's children have been delivered out of the darkness into his marvelous light. For them, the Satanic spell has been broken. Jesus is the Spell-breaker!

But once again, let us look back at the early years of mankind and make note of some significant developments such as: The first recorded death. It was not Able.

Okay. Wait a minute you say, and very quickly, you conclude: this must be a trick statement because there were only four living people at that time: two brothers and their parents. There was Adam, Eve, Cain and Able. You know that Cain killed his brother Able and that this was the first death and the first murder. But the truth is that this was not the first death, nor was Cain the first murderer.

Fact is, that the first murderer was not human. He is a spirit. And he was identified by our Lord Jesus Christ in Saint John 8:44 where he called the devil "a murderer from the beginning." And the first murder victims were Adam and Eve. Obviously, they did not die right away physically. We are not certain how long Eve lived, but we are told that Adam lived 930 years.

Now, God told Adam in Genesis 2:17 that "in the day that he ate of the tree of the knowledge of good and evil, he would surely die......In the day! Of course, neither Adam nor Eve died physically on that day, but at the very moment they partook of the fruit, they died spiritually and set death's relentless campaign in motion.

Satan had just committed his first double murder on planet earth! From that point on, there would be an ever-increasing number and variety of violent acts occurring in the earth. Sin and death partnered to magnify the violence of an evil brother against his godly brother, as the spirit of Cain united with the wicked one. (1ˢᵗ John 3:12) The spellbinder was pleased with the results he had through his having gained access to the heart of Cain, whom he claimed as his own. As the human population increased in the earth, he and his hoard of wicked spirits would seek to duplicate his success. They would diversify their tactics and intensify their efforts.

While God was searching the hearts, and examining the thoughts of every living man, the devil and many other evil spiritual personalities were working diligently to corrupt them all. The devil saw the universal corruption of humans, and perhaps, thought to himself, "I have succeeded in spoiling God's blessing plan for these detestable humans." No doubt, he was delighted when he learned that God intended to destroy man from off the face of the earth. Could it be that he had succeeded in forcing God to "scrap" his plans for mankind? Well, obviously not! Grace would show up before judgement came! God found in Noah, a receptive heart and suspended worldwide judgement until he could settle him and his family safely out of harm's way. (Humanly speaking) Noah and his family "worked out their soul salvation", literally.

But God would indeed, destroy that race of humanity that had so corrupted itself. They had no desire for him. They were consumed by their own lusts and were enticed by evil spirits to whom they yielded themselves. They didn't even want to think about God, so God left them alone…. until the day of his judgement came.

Today, society at large is very much like it was in Noah's day; under the power of the same satanic spell. Deception is abounding. Cold love and cruelty are commonly demonstrated in our world. Faith in God has been uprooted in the hearts of many in favor of faith in man.

But those of us who trust the word of God to be the foundation of truth, are not surprised about abounding iniquity and the love of many for God, turning cold. In Luke 18:8, Jesus seems to be considering the future and put forth this question: "When the Son of Man comes, will he find faith in the earth?"

Well, I can't speak for anyone else but if I am still alive on the earth at that time, I'm saying, Yes Lord, you will. And I trust, child of God, that you are saying the same thing. The spell is broken over our lives. We have responded to the divine invitation, and God has saved us out of this corrupt world. We are not settlers. We are pilgrims; strangers, nomads; in the world, but no longer of it.

The Spell-breaker has broken the shackles off our minds; taken the blinders off our eyes, and put the good news of the gospel in our hearts and our mouths to share with a perishing world. We pray God will use our witness to win more lost sinners to him. We were once one of them, but God put a saving word in the mouths of his servants and sent them to us. Today, we love him because he first loved us. Blessed be the name of the Lord forever and ever!!!

CHAPTER 7

The Living Experience

Human Imaginations of Divine Reality

Have you ever tried to visualize God in your mind as a "Person?" I have attempted to do so many times and for many years beginning all the way back at some point in my childhood.

Whenever the concept of "God" was awakened in my young mind, it was at that point that my imagination of Him was also awakened. As an immature youth with very little understanding or experience in the natural world, my imagination was limited, but always colorful. The best I could envision was a gigantic semi-invisible being taller than everything on earth including the mountains. I could see Him in my imagination walking around the earth looking down on all of us……. watching. Perhaps if I could concentrate deep enough on Him, He would let me see Him. "He's not completely invisible; He's only semi-invisible;" I thought. "If I just stare hard enough into the thin air, His image will appear," I thought. "But then again, do I really *want* to see Him?" "Maybe I'll die if I do!" After all, He likes you if you're good, but He's gonna get you if you're bad. "I ain't so good sometimes so maybe I better just let Him be."

What childhood images of God were produced in your mind? Was He the great invisible magician who gave all the circus magicians the "power" to pull a rabbit out of a hat?

Was he the father of Hercules; or maybe Superman's dad; or in your imagination, was He just a very, very old man? Was He the one who supplied Santa Claus with all the toys? After all, Santa was watching you too; you know; to see whether you were naughty or nice.

There is much wisdom to be gleaned from the immature perceptions of a child. And while we may chuckle with amusement at the simple "theology" of children, we should ask ourselves how different is our theology today? Many will discover that their rudimentary perceptions have changed very little. Others might come to realize that in "growing out" of childhood beliefs, they have also abandoned any serious considerations of the reality of God.

Still others have, at some point, arrived at the conclusion that God is real, but not relevant. Therefore, these individuals have "assigned" the "Lord of all" to an isolated "sanctuary" somewhere in the "far regions" of their minds to be called upon only when they are in trouble; and only as a "last resort." There are also those among us who, as we have discussed, openly practice those things that directly defy His revealed will, yet boldly declare themselves to be "Christians."

Conversely, there are those who seek to avoid ever talking or thinking about God because if they did so, the lifestyles they practice would convict their consciences with guilt and shame. Additionally, some have set out on a mission to silence the voice of conscience once for all by disproving God's existence, declaring that they owe no allegiance to any Supreme Being.

Vain opinions and wrong choices about God have produced grievous consequences of misery and suffering throughout all human history. While deceived men consider themselves to have grown up from their childish perceptions of God, the fact is that they have not really grown up; they have simply "grown away." For in many ways, the elementary perceptions of some were much closer to the truth than their "mature" fabrications.

Let us revisit our childhood perceptions for a few moments. Please allow me to use my own example to illustrate some notable considerations, because I can still remember some things I felt about God back then. I have already shared with you some idea of what I imagined God to look like. I expressed in brief, what I thought of God and what I thought God thought of me.

What I have not shared with you is how what I thought affected my actions and choices.

As a child, I thought of God often.

I believe that an obvious contributing factor to this was that God was often spoken of by my grandmother who, along with my grandfather, raised me from age one and a half. My great grandfather, who also lived with us until he died when I was around twelve, was a preacher. He taught me to memorize the names of the books of the Bible. My aunt Essie who lived next door was a Seventh Day Adventist who took me to Sabbath School many Saturdays during much of my early years. Then on every Sunday, my first cousin (who was more of a big brother, and is a pastor today in California) and I had to go to Sunday school and Church. Periodically, my grandmother would host a Women's Bible Study group at the house and everyone would bring a covered dish. Those elderly women would be in the front room praying, singing, testifying, crying, and worshipping.

As a young lad, I didn't think much of it back then, but I <u>do</u> remember wondering what that strange, warm peaceful feeling was that permeated the atmosphere in the midst of them? Later I would learn that it was the presence of God's Spirit.

Then, there was a young man who came to live with us (who is also currently a renowned pastor in Kansas City, Missouri). We grew into young adulthood as brothers.

My grandmother used to make he and I sing at some of their meetings.

Now I could go on daydreaming and reliving my childhood memories, but I will spare you. The point is, my mind was exposed to the consideration of God's reality early in my youth and it had a profound influence on the shaping of my opinion of Him. At the same time however, there were some deeply-rooted feelings that would not be altered for some time that was yet to come.

In all those years, there was a sense of inexplicable kinship to Him that I felt; a sense of longing to know Him. Yet equally powerful, was a sense of dread and alienation. Something in me believed that He loved me, but something else in me was always ready to flee at the thought of God coming near to me. I was a habitual liar as a youth and oft times, very angry on the one hand, and though often hiding behind false bravado, very fearful on the other.

Now we all have our story, but here is the point that I wish to arrive at, and the reason for sharing a small portion of mine.

- ***There is something inbred within the human soul that senses a kinship to something unseen; some hidden reality from which it is somehow detached and longs to be connected.*** (I sensed this as a child)
- ***There is something <u>else</u> residing within us that "instinctively" flees from the consideration of "accountability" to an unseen authority above us.*** (I sensed this also, as a child)
- ***The fact is that fallen man wants <u>a god</u>, but they don't want <u>GOD.</u>***

Mankind has always wanted, or *felt compelled* to pay homage to, "a god." That is the reason that since the earliest times, men have practiced idolatry; they have always been more willing to worship and serve a god they could conceive and construct in their own minds.

Fallen man rejects **the true God revealed** in favor of the "*fabricated*" *god imagined!*

So then, the fact is that in my case, my childhood perceptions of God did not change significantly from my early youth until age 20 when I received Jesus as my Lord and Savior. Before then, all my religious upbringing and influence had not removed my conflicting sense of kinship and alienation.

I am certain that many readers whose upbringing was completely different can still relate very intimately with the feelings I have described. *This is because I am identifying a universal truth.*

The natural human feelings of alienation from God are appropriate; for man in his unregenerate state, is *indeed*, both *conditionally* and *positionally* separated from God. He may attempt to compensate for this by constructing idols but:

- *What man "determines" God to be does not affect who He really is!*

("I am the LORD." "I change not" …….) Malachi 3 6

- *Man's rejection of accountability to God does not free him at all.*

("Every man shall give account of himself to God.") Romans 14 12

Here is the inescapable and eternal truth of the matter: **God Is!**

("Even from everlasting to everlasting, you are God") –Psalms 90 2

Without God, life is truly An Unsolvable Mystery.

But it seems that most human beings are too busy living out their lives to deeply consider its true meaning and purpose. Many have thought about it to some degree from time to time and have concluded that *life's essential meaning and purpose is an unsolvable mystery.* Where such is the case, there is perhaps, no motivation in the heart to further investigate the matter personally.

Instead, many have resigned to trust the opinions of those they deem wiser than themselves to sort it all out while they simply go on living. Those indifferent souls have become *blinded travelers on a spiritual journey, trusting their future to* those who are often no more able to provide satisfactory answers than themselves. In such cases, those trusted have become nothing more than *blind guides.*

And then there are others who are in thoughtful pursuit of answers to these elusive and multi-faceted questions on the meaning of life. Many conclusions have been arrived at among men. *But we all look for what we long for.* It is a characteristic of the human nature. Jesus puts it like this:

"Where your treasure is there will your heart be also."
(Matthew 6 21)

Many contrasting' and conflicting schools of thought have been developed drawing numbers of believing adherents. There is no universally accepted philosophy of life; but many popular views.

Much of the highly complicated, vastly speculative so-called scientific research about the origin of life is what the Bible describes as the "wisdom" of this world, which God deems as <u>foolishness</u>. (1st Corinthians 3 19)

So then essentially, life continues for many to be an unsolvable mystery the answer to which they have never been fully satisfied. The Bible speaks of people who are "ever learning but never able to come to the knowledge of the truth." (2nd Timothy 3 7) And so it is in our world. The tragedy is that multitudes of people have come to rely on the "experts" to sort out this increasingly more complicated experience we call life. Unfortunately, for so many, satisfactory conclusions have been delivered to them by errant messengers. And it is the "experts"; the "authorities" who have the power to sway collective human thought and belief. If what they believe is wrong, many others will be misled by their influence.

Certainly, all of us know that there is something greatly amiss in our troubled world; and the "experts" have not found the answers to our most pressing human needs. It seems that the more we learn and apply solutions to problems, the more we discover that our solutions become the seeds of a whole new crop of fresh problems. (... "ever learning but never able to come to the knowledge of the truth.) To this very day, so much that man claims to know is upon close scrutiny; purely theoretical.

Many proud scientists would have us believe that all phenomena can be described in principal, in terms of mathematical calculations, and that the material world is simply a measurable mechanism.

They go on further to say that humans are complex sub-mechanisms (machines, if you will) whose ***will*** and ***emotions*** are nothing more than *"patterns of chemical interactions among molecules"*. For the most part, in their world there is no need for, nor recognition of God.

<u>But they consistently fail the multitude of the members of the human family who continue to blindly rely on their "wisdom" to make sense out of life.</u>

Many were convinced during the time of the industrial revolution that humanity was sailing smoothly towards a utopian existence. But we have watched it come and go yet we still have not landed upon the shores of Utopia.

Undeniably, advanced technology has done much good in making use of the elements of our world to make life more comfortable for a percentage of the world's population, yet almost a billion people in our world today are hungry.

Many of our medical cures have side effects worse than the thing being treated.

And new diseases continue to surface more rapidly than medical science can deal with them.

The possibility of nuclear holocaust is ever looming over our heads.

But how is it that the experts continue to fail? Why can't they find permanent solutions to our problems that do not create new ones? Why can't we humans "get a grip" on life? The fears and insecurities that divide us; the hostilities that destroy us; the unpredictabilities that confuse us seem to have no end in sight.

The experts; the "great minds" among us have failed us in many ways because man cannot "think" his way out of his dilemma.

Nevertheless, many who bow to the "god" of reason scoff at the suggestion of any sort of unseen reality. For they fail to see that *reason itself must rely upon an unseen principle to function.*

<u>Reason is a faith-based principle</u>

But should we follow the process of natural reason to arrive at *every conclusion of life?*

Are there no boundaries or limitations to reason? Is it the supreme faculty of discovery within us to the exclusion of all others?

If so, then it must be able to stand alone, and I declare to you that it cannot.

Human reason cannot even function at all independently of other faculties.

We can neither believe in God nor atheism; creationism nor evolution purely based on reason alone. This is because *our reasonings must be supported by the higher principal of faith.*

Faith is not only the foundation upon which reason is built; it is the framework that holds it together. Only faith can bring our reasonings; individual or collective, into the realm we identify as reality.

I go to work for a company according to what I consider reasonable terms of employment. The company representative has told me that I must work a week "in the hole" meaning without pay and that I must work a second week to be compensated for the first week. At the end of the third week, I am promised to be paid for the second week.

Now if reason is not based on faith, it must be based on certainty. I either *believe* a thing or I *know* it. But how do I *know* that I will be compensated at the end of two weeks of labor?

How can I be irrefutably certain? Yet it would be unreasonable for me to insist that I be paid before I do any work for I cannot be irrefutably certain that I will be able to do the work I agreed to do. What do I know for certain?

But the truth is that all theory; scientific or otherwise, is based on a belief in the unseen, for it is the unseen aspect of all theory that makes it *theory* in the first place. All theories contain the element of trust in that which cannot be directly observed or proven. For example: we may observe the human brain, but not the *mind,* yet *we all* accept that the mind *is.*

Who witnessed the alleged aging of the earth over millions of years? *Who* has ever witnessed any species *evolve* into another? *Who* observed the so-called "Big Bang"? Are not all these theories based on blind faith?

What observable evidence do these secular believers have? Their tangible evidence is so scant that we must call these secular "believers" people of "great" faith.

I contend that man is out of control because he doesn't realize that he never was <u>in</u> control. If there exists nobody higher than himself to look to, history has shown, as well as the forecast of the future, that man is indeed without hope.

Life has an Originator. **Only the <u>Original</u> Authority can be the <u>final</u> authority.**

It is this Original Authority that has made man a seeker and traveler and placed him on this spiritual journey.

Those who never come to realize the nature of the journey may pass through this life and never realize the reason and purpose for which they were here.

If man dismisses the fact of an intelligent designer, his Creator, the answer to the questions of reason and purpose fade out of existence.

If we just **are,** and there is no higher purpose for our being, then ultimately, nothing **really** matters. At the end of this earthly journey, we may only look back and find that it has all been pointless; a fundamentally cruel joke without a jester.

But here is a faithful saying worthy of universal acceptation: God is! And here is another truth that can be relied upon: We can know Him!

Questions about God's origin are useless. God is not a part of the beginning of anything. He is <u>before all beginnings.</u>

God is beyond time. He has an endless supply of it. He is not confined to, nor bound by any of its constraints. Time is simply one of the properties God inserted into the physical universe when He created it. The very purpose for which time exists has no personal relevance to a Being whose nature excludes such natural laws as birth, aging and death. God is neither old nor young nor aging. He transcends all this natural stuff.

The only thing our human reason can do for us in the understanding of this reality is to acknowledge that it is quite reasonable to believe it.

For in the end, man must finally accept that human reason is neither omnipotent nor infinite. *There is knowledge that simply transcends human capacities of understanding.* Much that cannot be arrived at through research may be known by divine revelation, but only to those who believe.

Without acceptance of divine revelation, man wanders about in the realm of empty speculation convincing himself of things he doesn't know.

The truth is, that it is foolish and illogical to believe that the material universe came into existence **from** nothing, (which by the way, would make it a supernatural event) <u>and</u> **by** no one <u>and</u> **for** no apparent reason!

"*The fool* has said in his heart, there is no God (Psalms 53 1) but *the spiritual man* is called to be a student of a higher science that "compares spiritual things with spiritual." (1ˢᵗ Corinthians 2 13) This is the life of faith.

<u>Science is no enemy to faith.</u> It should be clearly noted that true science <u>does</u> indeed supply us with true and practical knowledge. To be sure, true science is no enemy to biblical faith. In fact, so-called modern science may trace its roots back to the inspiration found in the Holy Scriptures.

It is a great misunderstanding to confuse the fact that while there are many enemies to the Christian faith within the scientific community, that science itself is an enemy.

The Bible declares that "The heavens declare the glory of God and the firmament shows forth His handiwork." Night after night utters speech and day after day shows wisdom" (Psalms 19 1)

In other words, God is speaking to us through His creation every day.

True science as practiced by faith-filled practitioners investigates the material world to understand how God has designed it to work.

The Bible also declares that: "the invisible things of Him from the creation of the world are clearly seen, being understood by the things that are made; even His eternal power and godhead; so that they are without excuse. (Romans 1 20)

Passages such as these have inspired and encouraged some scientific minds to pursue the understanding of the hidden realities that under gird the material world; ascribing its laws to the wisdom of God.

From the beginning of human history, man has been not only encouraged but commanded by his Creator to "subdue the earth" (Genesis 1 28)

The voice of trustworthy science has supplied its students with much information in support of what the children of faith have already concluded: "God **is.**" And all matter exists because of Him.

Before we move on, let us just take a page or two from the findings of some of the most fundamental scientific research.

Firstly, we must acknowledge that we cannot remove the law of Cause and Effect from any study that is identified as natural science. And the clear implications of this law ever point to the matter of "first cause."

Consider the <u>First Law of Thermodynamics</u> which states that "matter can neither be created nor destroyed under *natural circumstances*." This is a powerful statement with serious implications against the theory that rejects creation by *Supernatural means.*

Practically no one denies that matter exists, yet according to this scientific conclusion, it could not have come into existence under *natural circumstances.* Now purely based on logic, where do we go from there?

<u>Scripture supports the conclusions arrived at by obvious reason</u>. **("things which are seen were not made of things which do appear." (Hebrews 11 3)** The fact is that within the confines of time, God created space and matter.

It is also a scientific fact that there is no <u>new</u> matter or energy appearing anywhere in the universe, and that all existing matter and energy in the universe remains.

This law is known as the <u>Law of Conservation of Mass and Energy</u>. It may be converted from one state to another, but never destroyed. As I said earlier, life never stops being life.

Based on our acceptance of these facts, we must conclude that there are only two options for the origin of matter: it has either existed eternally, or it came into being at some point in the infinite past. It should be noted that nothing has *ever* been scientifically observed to appear spontaneously out of nothing. That is, because *"nothing" cannot produce "something."*

This is elementary logic. Matter did not "self-create"; nor did it appear out of nothing.

Newton's <u>Law of Inertia</u> declares that a body at rest will remain at rest unless acted upon by an outside force.

Nothing exists without a Creator. Nothing moves without a "Mover."

The universe did not come about by natural means. It was supernaturally created by a supernatural God, leaving the details of its origin beyond the scope of all science and human reason.

Man is only privy to the study of the laws of the material universe, and not to the supernatural means by which these laws came into being; i.e., the "determinate counsels of God."

The true natural scientists should continue to search out the meaning and purpose for the things which exist in this material world trusting fully in the divine revelation of scripture:

"In the beginning, God created the heavens and the earth."

It is the invisible God of the Holy Bible who has set the universe in motion and by whom all things consist. (Job 1 8) (Colossians 1 17)

It has been argued by some that this notion of God's existence was formulated out of primitive man's inability to understand the nature of the world around him. But this argument is in direct contradiction to the revelation of scripture. For the words of scripture assure us that it is the world around us in all its wonder, that allows us to clearly perceive the power and glory of the invisible God. As man examines the natural phenomena occurring in the world that surrounds him, the fact of the unseen reality of God is presented in a way that leaves him without excuse.

But let us not think that the present condition of mankind represents how God has always been perceived. According to the scriptures, there came a point of time in history when such a condition did indeed come upon nearly all the entire human race, but it was not so from the beginning.

Early in human history, the existence of God was a part of the universal consciousness. Although man had become a sinner, the moral laws of God speaking to him through the voice of conscience continued to remind him of God's reality.

But because sin was at work in him through his own lust, his desires multiplied and diversified. The conflict between his conscience and his lustful desires rapidly intensified. Every sinful indulgence weakened the conscience and strengthened sin.

When sin reigns in the heart, the conscience is deadened and hatred for God is birthed in the heart. No one can love sin and love God too. In early human history, there was no denial of God's existence; but rather, it was an increasing refusal to submit to Him.

As time went by, through the enticements of evil spirits, fallen angels and the sinful appetites of the flesh, idolatry and later, even atheism came into existence among humanity.

Today, atheists claim that there is no logical basis for believing in a supreme being but just the opposite is true. There is truly no logical basis for disbelieving in the existence of a supreme being.

To disbelieve in the existence of God is not a natural outgrowth of human reason; *it is earthly, but unnatural.*

It is earthly in that *such a philosophy exists only in the minds of deceived earthly men.* Yet, the "inspiration" that produced it is neither earthly nor natural, but the exploitation of the natural senses by a supernatural force. The Bible calls it "earthly, sensual, and devilish." (James 3 15)

Satan: The one whose existence is not believed in by many, has deceived mankind in general and atheists in particular.

He is called by many names in the word of God; the Devil, Satan, that old serpent, Lucifer, Beelzebub, etc. The Bible says that this wicked spirit has deceived the entire world. (Revelations 12 9)

For over six thousand years, man's greatest enemy has watched him; studied him, and devised supernatural weapons of destruction with which to imprison and destroy him. He is no little red imp with a tail and a pitchfork as imagined in the shallow minds of some. He is the deadliest of all of humanity's enemies. It is he who has grossly distorted the truth about life and hidden its most essential truths from the minds of men. He is the inspirational force behind all false religions. He is the originator of the greatest conspiracy of all universal history. His greatest ambition is to destroy God's plan for mankind by concealing truth from him, and replacing God's reality with many counterfeits. But all who seek God with their whole hearts will find him. He is not far from any who desire him.

CHAPTER 8

The Search for Truth

"What is truth?" This is the famously intriguing question asked by Pontius Pilate, the Roman governor presiding over the trial of Jesus.

Jesus had been accused of calling himself God by his truthful acknowledgement of sonship, as well as "king of the Jews." His conspirators were accusing him of blasphemy and treason against Caesar.

Perhaps Pilate just wanted Jesus to confirm or deny the facts that had been presented to him; or maybe the nature of the inquiry was more complex than that. It seems highly unlikely that when Governor Pilate asks the question: "what is truth," that he is merely asking for the definition of a word here. After all, according to the narrative, he didn't even seem to be expecting an answer to his question. He didn't wait for Jesus to respond. He simply arose and went out to the mob of Jewish accusers and said to them, "I find no fault in him at all." (John 18 38)

But then, maybe he was asking Jesus the deeper, more perplexing question: "How does one really determine what's true and what isn't?" Perhaps not really expecting an answer to such a question, he just moved on.

For in this world, much of that which is visibly seen is often neither clearly, nor rightly understood. Fact is; there are many things in this world that are not truly as they seem.

Indeed, we live in a world where multitudes of legitimate things are overshadowed or substituted with illegitimate counterfeits. We are often deceived into honoring people who covertly practice dishonorable deeds. Hidden motives often guide the actions of people who claim to be working in our behalf for our highest good.

Truth may be defined as: "What accurately represents that which is real." So then obviously, the opposite of truth is simply, "untruth" (What does not accurately represent that which is real.)

Here is a fundamental truth about life according to the systems of this world:

The entire world of unredeemed humanity operates under the controlling influence of Satan, the father of lies. He is called "the god of this world" (or, worldwide social system) (2nd Corinthians 4 4)

The word "world" as it is used here is translated "age" and it is used in this phrase to convey the following meaning: that the prevailing views, opinions and ideals; hopes, reasonings and aspirations are satanically-inspired. The entire social, economic, educational, philosophical and false religious systems of the world have been influenced by the work of this unseen enemy and the hordes of evil spirits that are subject to him.

While many acknowledge the undeniable existence of deceitful men, they concurrently reject the notion that there are unseen evil personalities; or spirits that engage human thought processes with the intent of deception.

Many who confess their belief in the reality of an invisible God, and identify themselves as "Christians" deny the reality of an unseen Devil. But the "father of lies" is well represented in the world by deceived human beings.

Too many fail to see the inconsistency of accepting as true, what the scriptures say about God while rejecting what the same Bible says about Satan; what Jesus himself testified concerning this enemy of humanity.

This wicked and powerful unseen enemy is most pleased to have as many as possible believe that the reports of his evil operations are merely the fictitious rants of ignorant and superstitious men.

There have been court cases where heinous crimes have been committed by people who have testified that "the devil made them do it." In some of these cases, the defense has been successful in convincing the jury that the defendant was insane.

Why? It is because the jury was persuaded that the defendant truly believed himself to be under the control of the devil. This, they considered to be insane.

The fact that mental and emotional maladies treated with medicine and/or psychological counseling often provide some measure of relief does not dismiss the reality of evil spirits. If for example, certain drugs may be prescribed that help people who suffer from depression, this does not prove that an "unseen oppressor" does not exist.

The hidden mysteries of life and reality extend much further than the material-based reasonings of natural men. Don't reject the possibility of a thing simply because it is strange to you. The fact is: truth is stranger than fiction.

I wonder how many deceitful acts have been committed around the world over the last sixty minutes. I suspect that if there was a way to find out, the number would be astounding! How many lies told; how many thefts? How many false promises made; seductions; brain washings; propagandas? How many over the last twenty-four hours? Now consider the power of the lie:

Firstly, we should realize that the lie has become a common utility universally employed by the human family; young and old; rich and poor; people of every race, religion, or ethnicity. It is the height of naiveté to believe that everybody loves truth.

We categorize the lies we tell and give them labels such as "white" or "black"......... (I will resist further comment on that one.) We call some lies "good, or necessary." How often do we express what we truly believe? How often do we compromise what we believe to be true under the pressure of opposing opinions?

We sometimes acknowledge lies under the cover of deceitful synonyms: "I misspoke" takes the place of "I lied" or "I made a mistake". Well perhaps you speak truly if you are acknowledging the fact that the decision to lie was a mistake, but was the false speech itself a mistake; or was it a lie?

Then there are the so-called "innocent lies" of children:

Mother follows a crumb trail into Billy's room and asks: "Billy, did you eat that piece of cake I told you not to touch?" Billy, with chocolate on his fingers, crumbs on his shirt and a milk moustache quickly; wide-eyed, and with a look of surprised amazement answers: "Um No!" He is not a skilled liar yet; even as none of us are at first; but time and circumstances will continue to challenge him even as they continue to challenge us all.

Many people have allowed the pressures of life to turn them into chronic liars; many have not, and take great pains to be truthful and forthright in nearly all our dealings. But none of us have always been honest. In some places, the lie has found us all. (Even Abe Lincoln, no doubt.)

There is nothing humans privately espouse and publicly disown more than a lie.

There is, in our corrupted human nature, something that secretly love lies because they are quick, powerful and convenient resources that often provide easy escapes from uncomfortable (though often necessary) situations that we don't want to deal with. We lie to ourselves and we sometimes lie to others. There is no greater deception than when one deceives one's self.

There is an undeniable range of magnitude between the consequences of one lie to another. Lies are sometimes used with the intent of making the persons being lied to; feel better about themselves or their situation.

Then, there are horrific lies that produce immeasurable and irreplaceable loss such as the Iraqi "weapons of mass destruction" reports.

Lies are employed to recruit terrorists; many of whom have been deceived into thinking that in the murdering of innocent people they are serving God.

When lies are accepted as truth, people make incorrect and destructive decisions. These people will often be on the wrong side of an issue that is right and just. Conflicts of every sort erupt all over the world initiated by people acting on lies.

So then, how important is truth?

There is not a more noble and necessary pursuit in life than the search for truth. In a world engulfed in the moral darkness of falsehood and deception, truth is mankind's only beacon of hope.

So again; what is truth? This is a powerful question. For without truth, there is no right understanding of the meaning and purpose of anything in life.

Let me say that in life, it has been proven possible for one to have a multitude of facts and still be unable to uncover the truth of a matter. In the process of sorting out all the facts available, how do we intellectually flawed; emotionally biased, morally corrupted finite creatures ever come to discover the truth? Perhaps this is what Roman Governor Pontius Pilate was really asking Jesus. It is a powerful question.

There are many who have concluded that there is no such thing as absolute truth, but that all truth is only relative. There are others, myself included, who believe that all truth is absolute. There is no need to deny the fact of relativity in order to acknowledge absolute truth.

If by absolute, we mean: "that which perfectly embodies the nature of a thing." then whatever is *relatively* true is *also absolutely*; or perfectly true within its own context. If we have reason to believe that anything is true, we have reason to believe in absolute truth.

Truth is the manifestation of reality; or reality revealed. I am speaking here to the person who has only considered those things that can be seen, tasted, touched, smelled, or heard to be real.

I am telling you that the Ultimate Truth; (or Reality) of all things abides both inside and outside of the realm of tangibility; or materialism. In other words, there is tangible evidence all around us that point us to the intangible reality commonly known as God.

Everything is true within its own context; or realm of existence however, the fact is, Ultimate Truth permeates all things both visible and invisible.

I am telling you that all things are contained within Ultimate Truth, and that ***Ultimate Truth is a person***. Essentially, He is the only Person and He cannot be "contextually contained."

All things contain Him who contains all things. This is Ultimate Truth. ("In Him we live and move, and have our being." – Acts 17 28) yet, on the other hand; all things contain Ultimate Truth. ("And he is before all things, and by him all things consist."-Colossians 1 17)

God who is Himself, Ultimate Truth, fills all time and space. Therefore, ultimate truth is not a designation assigned by man; it is the other way around. Man's designation has been assigned by Ultimate Truth. We are; but we have not always been; but our Source has always been. From whence then, have we come?

For what purpose are we here? To what end shall we arrive? These are the fundamental questions of life. These are questions whose answers belong to the realm of faith.

The truth is that the philosophical roots of scientific research have been grounded in the task of solving the problems of natural life and discovering new horizons that clarify and expand both its meaning and possibilities. In and of themselves, these are noble pursuits.

What needs to be understood is that while science must inescapably utilize the principle of faith, it does so while comparing tangible things with tangible. But while the emphasis of science is upon reason, faith is involved in the entire process. It is faith that makes reason itself reasonable.

Whatever man has proven and accepted to be tried and true was first inspired within the faculty of faith-based reason and then motivated; empowered and sustained by that faith.

A primary dividing line between science and religion is drawn based on their difference in the recognition of inspiration.

Science seems to recognize inspiration as simply a human quality having neither origin nor supply outside of man himself. For most scientists, inspiration is no evidence of divinity because the existence of divinity can neither be "scientifically" proven, nor disproved.

There is however, a "deity" to whom many of them pay homage; it is, for them, the "supreme authority" of human reason. For the clear majority of them, all mysteries of truth and reality, if they are to be discovered, will be discovered within the scope of natural human scientific investigation.

Religion, on the other hand, interprets life based on whatever "theological system" it has embraced. Most people of monotheistic faith; that is, faith in only one supreme being, believe that all life's mysteries are contained within the mind, will and purpose of whatever deity in whom they have believed.

The gulf between science and religion is widened in the case where neither holds the other in a proper place of recognition. Cold, man-centered, reason-based science "dismisses what it sees as the "superstitious surmisings" of those who believe in the "inspiration of a deity." There is for them, no recognition of a god whose existence cannot be scientifically proven. In this sense, the practitioners therein along with others of this persuasion have in a sense, become "gods unto themselves." In such a case, morality itself is, of necessity, accordingly, subject to, and defined by them. Dismissing the existence of divine inspiration, they promote and propagate that which is "proven" to them to be true. This they do without any realization of the earthly, sensual, devilish motivations of unseen enemies by which they themselves are often inspired.

On the other hand, emotion-based, empty-headed religion often promotes the notion that faith and reason have no kinship to one another. This is the reason that so-called "divine inspiration" may be presented by deceived messengers who lead multitudes of gullible, hope-filled disciples down paths of error and destruction.

Let me reiterate emphatically, that there is a great supernatural deceiver of mankind who rules over a vast army of wicked spirits whose greatest weapon is "the lie." And let me say it again in the words of scripture: "THE ENTIRE WORLD is under the control of (Satan) the evil one." (1st John 5 19)

The collective mind of humanity is under the sway of its greatest enemy.

It is only the influence of the Holy Spirit of God and the remaining light of conscience in sinful man that restrains him and allows him the capability of inconsistent moral behavior. There is a constant conflict within the minds of all who are not in a state of reprobation; or complete union with evil. There are those who are indeed, willfully in complete union with evil.

On the other hand, there are holy angels; servants of the true and living God. Some are warring angels, and some are messenger angels. These powerful spirit beings oppose evil spirits and protect members of the human family according to the commands of those higher angelic authorities ordained of God to whom they are subject.

Please understand the territory that each side wants to control: It is the heart; i.e.; the mind of man. God desires to rule in our hearts through our free-willed surrender to Him in love. He desires to bestow upon man unimaginable joy and blessing through man's trust and obedience.

Our enemy, the devil would deceptively "befriend" man only to enslave him and ultimately destroy him by leading him to eternal damnation; a state he is already in, which is the destiny of those who are finally rejected of God.

This conflict, by its very nature will continue until the revelation of Ultimate Truth is manifested to all.

There seems to be at least as many earthly-minded, spiritually-dead adherents to religion in the world as there are openly secular human beings. Indeed, man's problems are rooted in his deceived self-perception and pursuit of independence. And all of humanity continues to experience the consequences of these misguided pursuits. It matters not whether intentional or unintentional, the consequences remain.

So then, the crux of man's problem lies at a deeper place within him that cannot be accessed through the mere powers of human reason.

Natural man's greatest hindrance to solving his problems is misplaced faith.

Scientists and secular man have exalted reason and rejected revelation. Natural man knows something is radically wrong with him and he mistakenly believes that he can "fix" himself and his world. He is ever learning, but never able to come to the knowledge of the truth.

He is a moral creature, yet he acknowledges either no absolute moral authority, or the wrong authority to whom he will be subject.

He wrongly assumes that he clearly knows right from wrong; good from evil; and such is not the case. And even the things that he knows to be right and wants to do, he finds himself unable to consistently do. He is a morally-wounded intelligent creature who was never designed to "direct his own steps" without inspiration from the Unseen Reality; the true and living God.

So many self-deceived individuals are under the delusion that humanity is fundamentally good. This simply is not true. The world is in moral chaos and the reason is because humans, although capable of doing some good, are incurably infected with evil. The world is not in the condition that it is in because we humans are good!

Unbelievers often seem to think themselves to be profound in asking very simplistic questions such as: "If there is a God, why does He allow evil to exist?" The inference is that if there is a God, there should be no evil.

The statement further and more deeply, presumptuously assumes to know the nature, purpose and responsibility of a God whose very existence is in question to them. They arrogantly may or may not allow for the existence of God, but if they do, He will be a god of their own moral and intellectual design.

It is because of the corrupted nature of man that he is blind to the necessity of the humility through which Ultimate truth may be found. In the book of Jeremiah, the 17th chapter verse 5 it reads: "This says the LORD; cursed [be] the man that trusts in man, and makes the flesh his arm, and whose heart departs from the LORD."

After having read this passage, some will laugh at the suggestion that man himself is not capable through his own pursuits, of eventually arriving at the ultimate reality. But finite, morally-corrupted man cannot rightly perceive himself as the summit of intelligence and from that vantage point; pursue those things that are higher than him.

Deeply consider the words of the Apostle Paul in **1 Corinthians 1 19 thru 29**:

(19) As the Scriptures say, "I will destroy the wisdom of the wise and discard the intelligence of the intelligent."

(20) So where does this leave the philosophers, the scholars, and the world's brilliant debaters? God has made the wisdom of this world look foolish.

(21) Since God in his wisdom saw to it that the world would never know him through human wisdom, he has used our foolish preaching to save those who believe.

(22) It is foolish to the Jews, who ask for signs from heaven. And it is foolish to the Greeks, who seek human wisdom.

(23) So, when we preach that Christ was crucified, the Jews are offended and the Gentiles say it's all nonsense.

(24) But to those called by God to salvation, both Jews and Gentiles, Christ is the power of God and the wisdom of God.

(25) This foolish plan of God is wiser than the wisest of human plans, and God's weakness is stronger than the greatest of human strength.

(26) Remember, dear brothers and sisters, that few of you were wise in the world's eyes or powerful or wealthy when God called you.

(27) Instead, God chose things the world considers foolish to shame those who think they are wise. And he chose things that are powerless to shame those who are powerful.

(28) God chose things despised by the world; things counted as nothing at all, and used them to bring to nothing what the world considers important.

(29) As a result, no one can ever boast in the presence of God.

In these passages, there is much to be gleaned concerning the distinction God has made between the wisdom available in this natural world and that wisdom which is revealed to the people who by faith, have heeded the call; or invitation of God.

The heart of this difference may be recognized by those who understand the difference between "*vain wisdom*"; or the wisdom of this world" and "*spiritual wisdom*"; the wisdom of God".

Let's consider the "wise" and the "intelligent" people of the world according to the scriptures that we just read, and make some notes:

First, it is God Himself who is being quoted by the Apostle in these verses; and God indeed acknowledges the "wisdom" of the "wise" and the "intelligence" of the "intelligent". Considering this truth, we today, who believe the sacred writings of the holy bible must also acknowledge the many advances of science and recognize the amazing intellectual capacity with which man has been endowed.

But having said this, we must also acknowledge how prone to error all humans naturally are. Despite all that we humans recognize as positive progress among us, the entire world is so saturated with error. This fact is undeniable. It is not pessimism; it is indeed the reality of our experience in the world.

Nor can we deny the historical, relentless and universal existence of evil. Many have alluded to it as a reason to deny the existence of God. Others are happy to confess their belief in the existence of a "god" upon whom they may *blame* all their inadequacies and failures. But the key to the doorway of understanding life's underlying reality is neither to blame God nor to deny his existence.

Secondly, God decreed that He would destroy the "wisdom" of the wise and discard the "intelligence" of the intelligent.

Alright, so think about this: It would be foolish to suggest that there is no present benefit in the practice of nourishing the body with food and drink, but when I am dead, this same concept will for me, no longer have any meaning whatsoever.

On the other hand, if I were never going to die, and the present state of the world was to remain the same indefinitely, then clearly, the necessity of body nourishment would be an eternal truth.

Now, we may see why human wisdom; or the wisdom of this world is vain; not because it is presently of no use or value, but because in the end, it will all be done away with. It has no enduring future.

So then, there is no enduring relevance to the godless philosophies; the scholarly dissertations, or compelling arguments and debates which may astound the world today. "The day will come", says God, "when they all shall be brought down to nothing."

But thirdly; and most importantly, God (the Ultimate Truth) has determined that He will conceal Himself and never be revealed to anyone by way of human reason or logic.

Do the "wise" fools of human intelligentsia propose to reduce the complexity of the divine nature to that which may be subject to human analysis?

Will man someday stand before his Maker; look Him face to face and proudly say to Him, "I've got you and your universe all figured out."?

Such a thought is not even worthy of consideration, yet attempting to arrive at ultimate truth by way of human reason apart from God's self -revelation is the equivalent of such human foolishness.

Even in man's search for truth, he is often, only searching for the truth he likes. In the movie, "A Few Good Men", there was a scene where actor Jack Nicholson was being pressed while on the witness stand to "tell the truth". He finally blurted the fiery response: "You can't handle the truth!" Those words represent a classic portrayal of what is true about morally-depraved human nature; it can't handle the truth.

That is why God can hide the truth in plain sight of those who trust in the wisdom of man. Indeed, in his pursuit of vain wisdom, man stumbles over the truth of God time and time again.

There is goodness in humanity, but that goodness has been tainted with evil. If I were wearing a white tee shirt with smudges on the back of it, but it was clean on the front side; would you call the tee shirt clean or dirty?

Do you always tell the truth; the whole truth and nothing but the truth under all circumstances? Do you know anybody who does? Of course, you don't. (Perhaps you are only seeing the front side of the tee shirt.) How would you even know? This is the point I make.

We must understand truth in more than terms of mathematical or scientific accuracy. Truth transcends facts. Truth is first and foremost a moral entity. That is why science cannot divorce itself from morality without becoming corrupt, for the very laws that govern nature are morally-based. They were designed to accommodate the well-being of the intelligent moral creatures that inhabit this planet.

The fact is: Love is the central law of the universe. A world perfected in love is a world perfected. And love is the Personality of Ultimate truth. That is why the scriptures tell us that God is love.

Life is a mystery that only its Creator fully understands. But God has made many truths available to a rebellious world of humans who are hell-bent on the pursuit of independence. The effect of this universal idolatrous quest has been the worldwide expansion of gross misinterpretation and misunderstanding of the rudimentary meaning of life.

Our depraved nature, originally born out of a desire for independence from the Creator has much to do with our limited ability to discern the difference between truth and error.

Why do conflicts of every imaginable sort abound among us, moving us to engage one another in one hostility after another? Why must peace on earth continue to be the fleeting aspiration that eludes all humanitarian endeavors? If experience has taught us anything, it has taught us that our faulty interpretations and choices have produced a history of tragedies that reach all the way back to our ancient beginnings.

What is truth?" To natural man, this is a tricky question, because we live in a world so full of falsehood and deception. We are sometimes, so easily misled. There is a collective naiveté and gullibility we are subject to simply based on the innate fallibility of our human nature.

"What is truth?" This is an important question because the effect of every choice we make will be based on whether we have arrived at it or not.

Truth is a Revealer. We must see that truth is related to reality. It is a revealer of reality and is often referred to as "light" in the Holy Bible. The fact is, truth and reality are inseparable. Truth, as it applies to us, is reality's meaning and purpose. Reality is the substance that always underlies the truth. Goodness is a quality of truth, but while truth itself is always good, the expression of it does not always manifest that which is good.

Truth does not produce good; it reveals it...Nor does it produce evil; it reveals it. Again; truth is not a producer; it is a revealer. Truth produces neither good nor evil, for truth is not the cause. It is our actions based upon our choices that are the cause behind the effects of moral good and evil.

Truth distinguishes good from evil. Falsehood may suggest: "Let us do evil that good may come of it"; but truth exposes the lie. God is real, but there many false gods & religions among the human family. Multitudes of false religions have recruited millions of followers all over the world. Many sincere believers have dedicated their lives to that which is untrue.

We as finite humans, find ourselves continually in search of answers to the questions that confront our lives. Countless times, in an endless number and variety of questions, we, like Pontius Pilate, have asked, "What is truth?"

Does truth really exist, or is life just an endless series of clues ultimately going nowhere; unanswerable questions taking us in circles as the years go by until we finally die never knowing why we were ever here?

What a sad and hopeless existence must they experience who subscribe to such a meaningless philosophy! In a world inundated with falsehood masquerading as truth; that which is real is often visible to us in an obscure or distorted representation.

Every finite, fallible human being born into this world has at some point, accepted and embraced many things that are not true. Because of this, many believe that truth is elusive, or worse; non-existent, but this is not so.

Is truth often distorted? Yes! Is it often concealed? Yes! Is it often rejected? Yes!

Truth is often concealed, but it is not hiding. Yet it has been hidden from those whose minds have been blinded by the supernatural enemy of mankind who uses our own vanity against us to deceive us. He secretly urges man to seek a "god" of his own imagination. He has appeared to many selected human agents as an "angel of light" and by deception, won their allegiance. These agents have in turn, promoted with conviction, that which is false. Thus, vain religions abound in a world system whose unseen ruler's hidden agenda is based on deception.

Miners search for treasures that are hidden in the earth. The oil; the silver; the gold; the diamonds; are all hidden and must be searched for, but they are not hiding. They do not relocate to some other part of the earth to avoid being discovered.

Nor does the truth, but it also must be searched for. God will reward them who diligently seek him. The archeologist does not pick up a shovel and begin digging randomly in the earth. After all, he is not simply on a quest to collect dirt, but he is in search of artifacts related to that which he has studied. He seeks verifiable evidence of that which history declares to exist. If he can locate it, see it touch it, examine and test it, he has discovered a truth. He knows it is true because he has experienced it. His discovery was not merely a result of blind luck. His earnest pursuit based on the right historical evidence combined with a wonderful spiritual thing called "inspiration" has led him to truth.

Considering the example of the archeologist, we too must earnestly desire and pursue truth based on the right historical evidence.

What truth do you seek? What historical evidence is there to make a case for it? And what is this inspiration of which I speak? The truth about life and reality from the God who brought it all into existence will be revealed to some, and concealed from many as He searches our hearts. His divine word is available to all, but received by relatively few. Truth itself is not hiding, but the God of truth is selective when it comes to those to whom He will reveal it.

The Bible tells us that the living God is no respecter of persons, which means that He does not "randomly" favor one person over another based on nothing but his sovereign power to do so.

He does, however, respect and conform to His own word. That which conforms to His word will find His favor. It is neither accidental nor incidental.

For example, salvation is available to all men, but only received by those who conform to the message of the gospel of Jesus Christ. No matter what else is claimed to be the saving power of God, the Bible says that: the gospel of Christ is the power by which God saves all who will believe. (Romans 1 16)

God did not foreordain that some be saved, and some lost, based on nothing but His sovereign authority to do so. Salvation is the collective operation of God that includes each person who individually chooses to believe the gospel of Christ. Jesus said, "Whosoever will, let him come and drink freely of the waters of life." But if a man will not drink, he will not have eternal life. Nor will any other spiritual truth be revealed to those who reject the gospel of Christ.

Here is wisdom for those who can receive it. Life is more than a mysterious phenomenon. Life in its essence, is a "Being; a Person. Life in its essence is eternal. Eternal life is God; or to put it in another way, God is eternal life personified. The "Supreme Being." (1st John 5 20)

God Himself is not only the source of life for all things, but He is the fundamental meaning and purpose behind all that is. Meaning and purpose can never exist apart from God. It has been settled in the heart and mind of this author that God is; and because God is, everything else is. He is Ultimate Truth. So then, for me, a proper pursuit of the meaning of life is a pursuit of God.

Jesus Christ provided the answer for us to the question Pontius Pilate asked when he prayed to God the Father in St. John 17 17. He said to the Father: "Thy word is truth." He admonished believers to seek; to knock; and to ask. Life is filled with meaning and purpose and it is ours, by divine permission, to inquire.

CHAPTER 9

God is!

"And without faith it is impossible to please Him, for he that comes to God must believe that He is, and that He is a Rewarder of them that diligently seek Him." (Hebrews 11 6)

The most rudimentary, yet comprehensive, elementary, yet profound statement that one can make about God is simply that He is. From the beginning of human history, God has distinguished the wise and the foolish from one another based upon their response to this truth. For the scriptures say: "The fear of God is the beginning of wisdom." (Psalms 111 10) The fool hath said in his heart "There is no God." (Psalms 51 3)

Every false philosophy of man is related to a misappropriation of that truth.

For example, some have altogether rejected the biblical account of creation; replacing it with mythology; or non-biblical theories such as Intelligent Design, or of course, Evolution, which promotes the idea of the eternity of matter.

Some believe that matter always was, and that over an extremely lengthy period, it simply *evolved* into the complex world we have today. They fail to see that such an idea does not even address the matter of life itself.

Instead of addressing the matter of life, they have become completely turned around in their thinking and are addressing the life of matter! They have somehow, come to equate a *product of life* with life itself.

It is easy to see how such a philosophy would spawn the mistaken idea that God and nature are one and the same.

Matter itself, has become to them, the source; the starting point; evolving and reproducing; a self-sustaining, chance-driven system with no divine operator.

These must oppose their own reasoning faculties to conclude that there is no need to consider a first cause.

According to this idea, all reality may be fully comprehended by the five senses of the soul.

So then, if they can't see it, taste it, touch it, smell it; or hear it, it cannot be proven to be real.

Apparently to them, *matter is all that matters*. But according to the Bible, the truth is that "matter" is not eternal; at least not in the sense that it always existed. It is the *product* of a reality that always was; that is immaterial; which is spirit.

There are two words available to us in accurately defining God with absolute certainty: God is. Over time, God has never "developed" or "evolved" in any way, but remains eternally, whom or what he is. His essential nature cannot change because the quality of his being is infinitely unchangeable. Nothing can be added to him nor taken away. He can neither be "improved" nor "diminished" in any way, nor by any means!

And in direct contradiction to the contention of many; **God, in his essence, is** *by human reason*, **undiscoverable**. Every thought of every human being from the beginning of human history to this very moment could not reveal His essential nature. There is nothing in nature; or the realm of human comprehension to compare it to. That is; in His inexhaustible, self-sustaining nature; the tracking of his utterly transcendent reasonings; the depth and magnitude of his eternal purpose.

Certainly, as Paul says in Romans 1 19 thru 20; there is within each of us that by which we may instinctively recognize invisible qualities of Gods' nature through the creation. And while these things manifest to us the infinite wisdom of God; all we can say about his essential nature is that "He is."

The fact is, that all who truly know God understand that what may be known of God is revealed by him; and that apart from this revelation, no one understands what makes him who or what He is.

Certainly, the realm of the spirit extends beyond the material world, and man was designed by his Creator to be conscious of it because, man's communion with God was designed to be Spirit to spirit.

Indeed, many are scarcely, if at all, aware of this inherent "higher sense" that supersedes those human faculties that give us consciousness of ourselves and the material world about us.

If a man cannot, or will not accept anything as real beyond that which can be accepted by his materially sense-driven intellect, he is blind to the tragically real problem existing within his being. He does not understand that he was divinely-designed to "see" beyond the realm of the visible; or material.

But this is where the divine design has been damaged. There is a problem with man's spirit and the injury has proven to be fatal.

As a result, his earthbound, materially-oriented *human nature* presides in the place that was designated for his *spiritual nature.*

In Genesis 6 3, God informs us that man had become "flesh".

Well…. what does that mean?

The short answer is that sin caused man to malfunction. He became "unplugged" from the true Power Source (God)

The Spirit to spirit connection with God was broken so that the desires of the body and mind have come under the power of sin. To say that man has become "flesh" is to say that he has come under the rule of his inherited sinful human nature. Lust has permeated the entire human family and is the dominate driving force behind human choices. He is flesh-driven; given over to his lustful appetites. He is neither totally bad nor good, but is "contaminated."

The problem is that the desires of the flesh are contrary to the desires of the spirit that was formerly in communion with God. It was the sin of Adam that caused the "disconnect". So now man has become "flesh".

Let's just go all the way back to the beginning and examine God's process in the making of man according to the book of Genesis:

1 26 "And God said, let us make man in our image, after our likeness: and let them have dominion over the fish of the sea, and over the fowl of the air, and over the cattle, and over all the earth, and over every creeping thing that creeps upon the earth."

1 27 "So God created man in his own image, in the image of God created he him; male and female created he them."

2 7 And the LORD God formed man of the dust of the ground, and breathed into his nostrils the breath of life; and man became a living soul.

Now let's break these verses down and see what can be gleaned from them, but before we do, let's get clarity on something that may otherwise, hinder us further down the road. It concerns the word "us" in verse 26.

First, God said: "Let us make man in our image, after our likeness.

Now regarding the question that immediately arises concerning the "us" in verse 26, it does not refer, as the Trinitarians believe, to "the second person" of the Godhead. Nowhere does the Bible even suggest that God is a group of three supreme beings who inexplicably are one. Jesus is not the "Eternal Son" in the sense that it has been so from eternity as he was clearly born at a specific point in history. Also realize that when God speaks of his personhood, he speaks in the singular.

Ok; so then why DOES God say "us" in that verse? Well, here is the scripturally supported answer to that question.

First, let's remember that God is sovereign; not subject to anything but his own will. (Exodus 3:14 And God said unto Moses: "I AM THAT I AM: (or; "I will be what I will be") and he said: "thus shalt thou say unto the children of Israel", (I AM) … hath sent me unto you."

So, let us not think of God (who will be whatever he will be) according to *human* terms and limitations. And while that is true, let us also, not take the liberty of "creating "a "god" of our own imaginary design. Let us use the scriptures so that God can tell us for himself who he is.

To understand why God says "us" in this verse, let us look at a few passages of scripture that will shed light:

(Genesis 1 1) "*In the beginning* God created the heaven and the earth".

(John 1 1thru 3) In *the beginning* was the Word, and the *Word was with God, and the Word was God.*

The same was in the beginning with God.

All things were made by him; and without him was not anything made that was made.

Now according to Genesis 1, God created the heaven and the earth.

According to John 11, the Word was with God and the Word was God.

Let's stop here and ask the question: Are we being told here that one God was with another God?

The verse clearly says that the one who is called the "Word" was God. It also clearly says that the one identified as "God" was with God. If as the scriptures indicate, God was with

God, were there then, two distinct "gods" there together? The answer is an emphatic "no". In Isaiah 44 8, God is speaking. Listen to his words: "Is there a God beside me? Yay. there is no God; I know not any ".

Ok, so maybe there is, as once again, the Trinitarians say, "a plurality of separate and distinct beings, or three *persons* within one Godhead." Do the scriptures support such an idea? Once again, the answer is an emphatic "no".

In scripture, the personhood of God is always spoken of in the singular tense. (Job 1 8) Will ye accept his person? will ye contend for God?

But now let's go to the first Chapter of Hebrews and carefully read verses 1 thru 10:

God, who at sundry times and in diverse manners spake in time past unto the fathers by the prophets,

Hath in these last days spoken unto us by his Son, whom he hath appointed heir of all things, by whom also he made the worlds;

Who being the brightness of his glory, and *the express image of his person*, (not "persons ") and upholding all things by the word of his power, when he had by himself purged our sins, sat down on the right hand of the Majesty on high;

Being made (not created) so much better than the angels, as he hath by inheritance obtained a more excellent name than them.

For unto which of the angels said he at any time, you are my Son, this day have I begotten you? And again, I will be to him a Father, and he shall be to me a Son?

And again, when he brings in the first-begotten into the world, he saith, and *let all the angels of God worship him.*

And of the angels he saith, who makes his angels spirits, and his ministers a flame of fire.

But unto the Son he (God) saith, thy throne, _O God_, is for ever and ever: a scepter of righteousness is the scepter of thy kingdom.

Thou hast loved righteousness, and hated iniquity; therefore God, even thy God, hath anointed thee with the oil of gladness above thy fellows.

And, Thou, Lord, in the beginning hast laid the foundation of the earth; and the heavens are the works of thine hands:

In these verses, we clearly see from verse 2 that God has spoken to us in these last days by his son whom he has appointed heir of ALL THINGS. This is because ALL THINGS were not only made BY HIM, but all things were made FOR HIM.

In verse 3, God says that his son is "the brightness of his glory"; in other words, the one thru whom his glory is manifested to all; AND "the express image" (or exact representation) of his person.

As humans, our physical bodies have been given to us as visible representations of the invisible selves we are. That which makes me who and what I am lives inside this physical representation called a body. I am a soul made visible thru the "house" (my body) I occupy.

I am a triune being composed of spirit (life principle), soul (personality) & body (habitat, or home).

These three elements of my being are separate and distinct OFFICES OR FUNCTIONS of my *singular* person. They obviously don't add up to three separate and distinct persons.

Nor is God three persons in one godhead. According to Colossians 1 9 (For in him (Christ) dwells all the fulness of the Godhead bodily.) Again; neither am I (who am made in his image and after his likeness) three persons in one body. All the fulness of who and what I am (my personhood) resides in this body.

One God ("I will be what I will be") has revealed himself in scripture as the Father, Word, and Spirit (1st John 5 7). When the Spirit of God infused the womb of the virgin with the holy life of God, the Word was made flesh; the one and only God inhabited in all his fulness, a sinless human body.

Thus, Jesus was, and is completely God and completely man.

So, by now, I trust that the light of truth has shined upon your understanding about who the "us" of Genesis 1 26 is. It is the Father and the Word; by the power of the Spirit; all components of his very being; his singular person in operation to "make man." He uses the "us" prophetically to cover both his divinity and his future humanity. Therefore, Paul said in 1ˢᵗ Corinthians 15 57: "The first man is of the earth, earthy: the second man is the Lord from Heaven."

*Now, let us proceed with our consideration of God's process in the making of man so that we may compare man as he was originally designed to what he became after the "fall" of Adam:

Once again, let's look at Genesis 2 7 "And the LORD God formed man of the dust of the ground, and breathed into his nostrils the breath of life; and man became a living soul ".

So then, since God shaped him from the dry earth; he is, in this sense, no different from the other earth-bound creatures that God had made before him. Also, part of the "breath of life" that God breathed into him is simply oxygen. Nothing about this makes humans unique; or different from any other land animal either. The verse goes on to say that man "became a living soul".

Now as far as the Old testament is concerned, the Hebrew word for soul is "nephesh" which is translated to mean: a person; a breath, a soul, or a life. According to that usage, living creatures (including humans), rather than possessing souls, are themselves, souls.

The nature of the soul is "spiritual" but not the same as "the spirit" because it is "earthly"; appointed to this temporary material world. It is subject to death. It cannot ascend to the realm of the Spirit to commune with God. It has a dual nature because *it was produced as a result of the union of spirit and matter.* God made man in his own image and after his likeness by instilling an immortal spirit within him thru his Word. This is what John is speaking of in chapter 1 about the Word that was with and was God, for he goes on to say in the 9th verse that he was the true light that "lights" (or; instills the immortal spirit in) every man that cometh into the world.

Because of this, before Adam sinned, he could commune with God spirit to Spirit. But the fact is that man did sin, and in so doing, lost both his innocence and his pure fellowship with God.

The invasion of sin into his human nature along with the assaults on his mind by unseen supernatural enemies caused him to be a morally fallen soul.

His spirit could no longer communicate divine inspiration and guidance to his soul.

His soul was designed by God to be the mediator between man's spirit and body.

Now instead of man being spirit-ruled, he has, through his soul, become sense-ruled.

His fleshly nature has become empowered thru the improper rule of the soul.

Thus, God says: "My Spirit will not always strive with man for that he is also, *"flesh."*

His spiritual nature has become subject to that over which it was created to reign.

Therefore, the natural man will continue to think naturally, and man-centered philosophies will continue to be birthed in his heart.

But uninspired, man-centered philosophy will never lead him to the revelation of life's true design and purpose.

The true meaning and purpose of life must be revealed to man by the One who provided it.

And God has awakened a generation of human beings who were spiritually dead and adopted them into His own spiritual family.

They are the born-again children of God; the "salt", or those for whom God would preserve the earth.

We who represent the "salt" cannot therefore, allow ourselves to be drawn away from a spiritual mind into a sense-ruled mentality that finds its "inspiration" in the carnal wisdom of the unregenerate intellectual world of natural man.

Indeed, it is possible for unregenerate men to know many things that are true about material life and reality without knowing God. The problem with this is that, as well as they know and believe some things that *are* true, they also, by uninspired human reason, believe much that is not true. To make matters worse, they build their world views upon the false foundations of these false philosophies. Nor can it be said that believers in the God & Christ of the Bible have gotten it all right simply because they believe in God, but if they have obeyed the gospel, they do have the fundamental truth correctly and that is so very important.

When men recognize the sovereignty of God, they rightly assign themselves to a place that can open the door to true revelation of the meaning of life.

If man sees himself as the central object of life, he has set himself in the place that belongs to God. Tragically, while improperly seated, he develops erroneous world views.

It is not that the philosophical foundations upon which these views rest are completely wrong, but when that which must be pure becomes tainted, it can never correctly serve the purpose to which it was assigned. Truth mingled with falsehood always misleads.

Without a doubt, the most deceptive things in our world are based upon half-truths. Gravely important matters are misconceived, inspiring false remedies; it's like having a headache and taking an aspirin laced with cyanide.

Many life philosophies have been established among men based upon universally accepted truths. The problem is however, that the conclusions of these universal truths are wrongly interpreted by those who place man at the center of life and reality rather than God.

The following is an example of a universal truth, the conclusions of which are wrongly interpreted thereby establishing a wrong world view:

I am alive today, but one day this body will die.

The fact of the historically witnessed eventuality of bodily death is beyond debate.

In other words, this is a universally recognized fact among us all.

Human values and life philosophies are established according to this recognized reality. *It is a right point, but a wrong starting point.*

The man who fails to *first recognize that "God is";* always begins to develop his system of beliefs from a wrong starting point.

An example of the effects of this premise may be seen in the practice of *hedonism. Hedonism may be defined as:* a doctrine that pleasure or happiness is the sole or chief good of life.

Our world is filled with people whose way of life is based on this philosophy.

But hedonism is a false philosophy of life that is at the root of so much of humanity's misery and confusion.

We must understand however, that Hedonism as defined here is clearly not entirely false. In fact, it is indeed true that pleasure or happiness is the chief good of life. For without pleasure, there is no desire, and without desire, there is no choice, and without choice, there is no action.

Without action, there is no life.

There is a spiritual nature in man that finds pleasure in things of which his defective human nature has no sensitivity as the pleasure principal in his human nature has become corrupted.

There is now within him desire for much that is evil and detrimental to his own well-being.

This being so, his ability to make good choices has been clouded and impaired by conflicting desires within him. His quest to find pleasure while infected with a corrupted moral nature has empowered lust to often preside over his moral choices. Even when he desires the right things, there are conflicting desires for the wrong things. When he would do good, evil is there present with him.

Alright then; so, we are convinced that pleasure is the chief good of life. Enter this truth, but do so at a false philosophical *"starting point"*: "I am alive today, but one day this body will die." Obviously, this is not a false point, but it is a false *philosophical* starting point. All philosophical starting points that begin with man saying: "I am" before acknowledging that "God is", are false philosophical starting points.

Now blend this fact in with *a lie*: "When I die, I will no longer exist." This is a philosophical aspirin-cyanide "cocktail" that induces spiritual death rather than life. If the death of my body did indeed, mark the end of my existence, then my own temporary pleasure in this world would clearly seem like the only reasonable pursuit.

But the truth is manifest to those who recognize God as the highest reality and His revelation as the foundation upon which the philosophy of all life and reality must rest.

The following is unmingled truth based upon the word of God:

- The death of my body does not mark the end of my existence. ("And as it is appointed unto men once to die, but after this the judgment." (Hebrews 9 27)
- There is an appointed time after physical death in this world that every man must give account of himself before God. (1st Corinthians 5 10)

Every man born will continue to exist after physical death, but the nature and quality of his existence will be determined by the choices he made during his earthly sojourn. On any journey, the traveler must do more than determine where he or she wants to go. Before the journey even begins, there must be a plan that involves time, means of travel, and all other details to successfully arrive at the desired destination.

Considering this future appointment with death, the true priorities of life must be established.

If one chooses not to believe the report of the inspired writers of scripture, time will prove such a choice to have been disastrous.

When values are set based on a wrong initial premise, the values themselves must necessarily also be wrong.

"Eat, drink, and be merry, for tomorrow we die" is a mistaken point of view about life that exalts the pursuit of temporary earthly pleasure to an inordinate place of prominence.

Consider this philosophy in the light of the life philosophy presented to us by the Lord Jesus Christ: (Luke 12 16 thru 32)

Verse 16. And he spake a parable unto them, saying: The ground of a certain rich man brought forth plentifully:

17. And he thought within himself, saying, what shall I do, because I have no room where to bestow my fruits?

18. And he said: "This will I do: I will pull down my barns, and build greater; and there will I bestow all my fruits and my goods."

19. "And I will say to my soul, Soul, thou hast much goods laid up for many years; take thine ease, eat, drink, and be merry."

20 But God said unto him: "You fool, this night thy soul shall be required of thee: then who's shall those things be, which thou hast provided?"

21. So is he that lays up treasure for himself, and is not rich toward God.

22. And he said unto his disciples; therefore, I say unto you, take no thought for your life, what you shall eat; neither for the body, what you shall put on.

23. The life is more than meat, and the body is more than raiment.

24. Consider the ravens: for they neither sow nor reap; which neither have storehouse nor barn; and God feeds them: how much more are you better than the fowls?

25. And which of you with taking thought can add to his stature one cubit?

26. If you then be not able to do that thing which is least, why take ye thought for the rest?

27. Consider the lilies how they grow: they toil not, they spin not; and yet I say unto you, that Solomon in all his glory was not arrayed like one of these.

28. If then God so clothe the grass, which is to day in the field, and tomorrow is cast into the oven; how much more will he clothe you, O ye of little faith?

29. And seek not you what you shall eat, or what ye shall drink, neither be ye of doubtful mind.

30. For all these things do the nations of the world seek after: and your Father knows that ye have need of these things.

31. But rather seek ye the kingdom of God; and all these things shall be added unto you.

32. Fear not, little flock; for it is your Father's good pleasure to give you the kingdom.

In these verses, The Lord informs us that the proper and foremost pursuit in life is the kingdom of God.

This truth corresponds quite naturally with the clearest sense of human reason.

If we are convinced in our hearts that God is the Creator of all things, and that He is the reason for our existence, then our highest pursuit ought to be Him.

The holy scriptures teach kingdom seekers the following truths:

A. All creation is subject to Him. He is Lord of all.
B. To seek the kingdom is to seek the will of the King.
C. If I discover and practice the will, or rules; or laws of the King, I will have discovered, and am living according to my purpose in His kingdom.
    Scripturally, this is called walking in the light.
    We who in simple faith, earnestly endeavor to practice such a lifestyle are called "children of light."

D. To discover my purpose and direct my life in keeping with that purpose will bring the Kings favor upon me.

E. To presume to discover my true purpose without regard to any pursuit of the will of my Creator is to live life without reliable direction. Those who embrace this attitude and lifestyle are scripturally called "children of darkness."

F. To disregard divine counsel and direct my own steps is to bring the Kings disfavor upon me and to classify me as a rebel and a member of a "renegade kingdom."

G. There are only two fundamental classifications of spiritual life and reality in this world: "light" and "darkness."

Listen to the words of the wise king Solomon: (Ecclesiastes 11 8 and 12 14)

8. But if a man lives many years, and rejoice in them all; yet let him remember the days of darkness; for they shall be many. All that cometh is vanity.

9 Rejoice, O young man, in thy youth; and let thy heart cheer thee in the days of thy youth, and walk in the ways of thine heart, and in the sight of thine eyes: but know thou that for all these things God will bring thee into judgment.

10 Therefore remove sorrow from thy heart, and put away evil from thy flesh: for childhood and youth are vanity.

12 1.

Remember now thy Creator in the days of thy youth, while the evil days come not, nor the years draw nigh, when thou shalt say; I have no pleasure (impotency) in them;

2. While the sun, or the light, or the moon, or the stars, be not darkened, nor the clouds return after the rain:

3. In the day when the keepers of the house (bones) shall tremble, and the strong men (muscles) shall bow themselves, and the grinders(teeth) cease because they are few, and those that look out of the windows (eyes) be darkened,

4. And the doors shall be shut in the streets, when the sound of the grinding is low, and he shall rise up at the voice of the bird(insomnia), and all the daughters of music shall be brought low;(deaf and toneless, quavering voice)

5. Also when they shall be afraid of that which is high, and fears shall be in the way (lack of balance and fear of falling), and the almond tree shall flourish (gray hair), and the grasshopper shall be a burden (void of energy), and desire shall fail (sex drive lost): because man goes to his long home, (standing at death's door) and the mourners go about the streets:

6. Or ever the silver cord be loosed, or the golden bowl be broken, or the pitcher be broken at the fountain, or the wheel broken at the cistern. (death arrives)

7. Then shall the dust return to the earth as it was: and the spirit shall return unto God who gave it.

8. Vanity of vanities, saith the preacher; all is vanity.

9. And moreover, because the preacher was wise, he still taught the people knowledge; yea, he gave good heed, and sought out, and set in order many proverbs.

10. The preacher sought to find out acceptable words: and that which was written was upright, even words of truth.

11. The words of the wise are as goads, and as nails fastened by the masters of assemblies, which are given from one shepherd.

12. And further, by these, my son, be admonished: of making many books there is no end; and much study is a weariness of the flesh.

13. Let us hear the conclusion of the whole matter: Fear God, and keep his commandments: for this is the whole duty of man.

14. For God shall bring every work into judgment, with every secret thing, whether it be good, or whether it be evil.

So then, in these two passages of scripture, two vital truths about life's reality are illuminated:

1. What is ultimately important in this temporary life is discovering by God's revelation, how He intends for us to live it.
2. On the other side of this life, we must all give account to God for how we chose to live the life He

gave us considering the truth He made available to us.

But doesn't everyone desire pleasure? Certainly, it is contrary to nature (both human and divine) not to. But we were divinely-designed to be God-centered; not self-centered.

It is not the desire for pleasure that is condemned in scripture; it is "the love of pleasure rather than the love of God." (2nd Timothy 3:4) It is a matter of priorities; the proper order of love's applications.

Let us be clear on this matter. Love originates from only one source; God.

It proceeds forth from the very soul of God, and is manifested in all His wondrous works.

It is God's good will towards the world in general and His children in particular.

There is only one way for men to *love God*. It is to *obey Him*. (John 14 15) (1st John 15 10)

(2nd John 1 5)

And there is only one way for men to *please God*. It is to *trust Him*. (Hebrews 11 6)

Also, we must understand that self-love is natural and according to God's design.

God loves Himself and pleases Himself. He made us in His own image and after His own likeness.

This means that we should love ourselves. By loving one's self, it is meant to take interest in, and pursue that which is good for one's self. How can we love others before we love ourselves?

God has given each of us a temporary earthly life that by nature, loves itself. While it is true that sin has caused this natural inclination to be destroyed in the hearts of many, to love one's self is natural. That is why we are commanded to love our neighbor as ourselves.

But an important thing to know is that love of any specific thing is not automatic. Nor is love of certain things inevitable. Love is a learned response and always a choice. It is like water in that it may be mixed with an endless number of things serving as the essential element or ingredient. Water mixed with dirt becomes dirty water. Love mixed with lust produces greed. Yet in both cases; love and water; there are countless good and necessary things that require them. In fact, both love and water are vital to the survival of life.

But the fact is that God has given us self-love as a model to examine so that we could prioritize our lives accordingly. The primary element of love is pleasure. Once we understand this, we must ask ourselves, "Who should we first seek to please?

When we love God first, the things that please Him will also please us.

This is because God finds pleasure in our greatest happiness and has designed true life accordingly.

Many fail to see God's wonderful provision for the children of men by that which all of nature provides. Man's every need has been provided by his Creator yet different men suffer lack in diverse ways all over the world. It is because mankind has not collectively loved the Creator.

Man has been deceived into loving pleasure (and money; the primary means of obtaining pleasure) ahead of; or instead of God.

But when we love pleasure first, we expose ourselves to powers greater than us who are in fact, rebels against the will and purpose of God. No good has ever, nor ever shall come of that for us.

Fallen man has been convinced that to love himself is the greatest love, and it has led to "self" becoming his only true love. He loves money; he loves pleasure because he loves himself first and foremost.

He wants what he wants. He has become self-willed.

The truth is, however, that the self-will practiced by man did not originate with him. He is a "pawn" being manipulated by powers greater than himself. (2nd Peter 2 11)

Some men love sports more than their families. It's true! There are many among us who love *things* much more than people.

That is why with multitudes of starving and homeless people in the world, many wealthy people are somehow, unable to feel any compassion. Many do nothing to relieve suffering in the world. Many will contribute to the saving of whales before the saving of infant and children. There are deeply compassionate and caring souls among the wealthy, but with many, no chord of compassion is ever struck in their hearts towards contributing to the aid of suffering fellow human beings

Of course, there will always be the greedy; the presumptuous; the opportunistic and unappreciative among us. There will always be sluggards among us who can provide for themselves, but prefer to prey on the charitable hearts of others. But we cannot allow this to birth in us contemptuous attitudes towards the poor lest we also become hardened against the legitimate suffering of the helpless among us.

In the heart that loves self more than the God who gave us selfhood dwells an idol by the same name; "self."

It is this self-centeredness that has ousted God from the place of sovereignty in the hearts of men.

This is the primary reason why self-centered humans become addicted to the need for immediate gratification of the senses and become enslaved to a plethora of harmful habits.

Can you see now why Esau was regarded as a profane man because he was willing to give up something as valuable and sacred as his birthright for a morsel of meat? (Hebrews 11 16)

The entire world has been corrupted through lust. (1st Peter 1:4)

But it is not the intense desires themselves that have corrupted the world; it is *what we desire*; it is what these intense desires stir our hearts to pursue. *What humans do to satisfy the lusts of their hearts destroys the purity of all things in the world.* The things provided by the Creator for our good are abused or misused and thereby corrupted or destroyed.

So many people in pursuit of pleasure live their lives without regard to necessary restraints. Countless men, women and children have become slaves to addictions that often destroy the lives of others as well as their own.

Often, a legacy of addictive behavior is passed on to the generations that follow.

The Bible identifies this tragic seed of destruction among the natural families of men as generational curses (Exodus 20 5) Such curses are said to extend to three or four generations.

How many marriages have been wrecked as sacred vows were abandoned and fidelity compromised because of unrestrained desire. How can faithfulness prevail in a marital relationship where either one or both partners hold self-gratification as the most important value of life? Loyalty and commitment cannot thrive in such an environment.

The true nature of love is self-giving, not self-gratifying.

Inordinate self-love has deceived many into thinking that they love the other person when the truth of it is that they are only *using* the other person as an *instrument* to love themselves. This is one of the greatest reasons why so many marriages fail, and divorce is epidemic.

To the hedonistic mind, if you cease to be a source of pleasure, you no longer are loved; which really means: you're no longer of any practical use. People and relationships are always dispensable to those who worship the false god of pleasure.

In America, to be a "star" athlete or entertainer is to be a god or goddess. When America considers you a star, your public presence in any setting makes it an "event."

If you write your name on anything when you are a "star", it becomes a valuable item.

Why does anyone in journalism or the television media think it important that we, the viewers know what the famous entertainers or athletes of our world did today? Why do such media outlets not only exist, but thrive? Why do we have "the paparazzi," a group of frenzied camera-loaded reporters nearly trampling one another just to get a picture or comment from these people?

It is because there is a huge market for such entertainment in a vain world; a vain nation such as ours. There are so many people of whom I have heard, having made no effort to learn of them.

What I have been told of them has provided nothing meaningful to me.

Yet many who have made the greatest contributions to the betterment of humans are by comparison, unknown to me by name. To learn of these valuable persons, I must do research.

This is because their work was not associated with the vain pleasures pursued by the hedonistic minds of pleasure-worshippers.

But it will not be the god of pleasure before whom all men must one day stand and give account.

(2nd Corinthians 5 10)

The world is filled with people who "believe in God." But to determine what a person means by believing in God requires a deeper investigation than taking such an utterance at face value.

If the god I believe in was created according to my own imagination based upon what I wished him to be, my "god" is also my possession. He is a "god" under my rule; after all, I created him.

Those who have created their own "god" say things like: "My god would never cause dreadful things to happen to anyone, or allow them to suffer eternal punishment; he loves everybody no matter what."

I agree with the people who say such things. What they are saying is absolutely true.

Others say things like: "Everybody has their own relationship with "their god"; it's personal and nobody can tell another person how they should serve "their god." Again, I couldn't agree more with them. If men "create" gods of their own design, they have the right to determine how these little gods should operate. These little gods are not reverenced or feared; their very nature and character is determined by their human "creators."

But the fact is that man's imagination *does not* and *cannot* produce reality.

In the 1960's there was a popular drug that was labeled a psychedelic drug called LSD. Some people "high" on that drug would imagine that they could fly. As a result, there were people who leaped out of windows at elevated heights to their deaths. Man's imagination; drug-induced or otherwise, *does not* and *cannot* produce reality. There are many "gods" in our world but there is only one true and living God. The true and living God is not subject to men's fantasies; nor is He careful not to offend men's opinions.

Spiritually dead men have no idea how inappropriate and arrogant their estimations of their own importance are in the light of the reality of God. The truth of God's existence is not dependent upon man's endorsement. He is who He is independent of all perceptions of Him. His providential care extends in many ways, to the just and the unjust; the believing and the unbelieving alike; for sunshine and rain both make their contributions to the children of men without partiality. (Matthew 5:45) He is the Uncreated Reality in whom we all "live and move and have our being." (Acts 17 28)

There are those who reject the reality of the biblically-revealed personality called Satan. But how can one accept the reality of the God of the Bible and reject the reality of Satan from the same Bible? If one rejects the authority of the Bible as the revelation of truth, the God in it must be rejected as well. There is no greater display of satanic deception than that uttered by the "fool" who says in his heart: "There is no God."

There is no greater blessing conferred upon the human soul than that which is bestowed upon those who by faith in God's self-revelation in scripture, joyfully declare that God is! There is not a statement more celebratory or eloquent than these two words: God is! Bless His Great name forever!

To believe in the existence of God is a matter of instinct born out of both the *spiritual* and *natural* human attributes of intuition, conscience, intellect and reason. In other words, *man has a built-in capacity that enables him to believe in the reality of a God he cannot see.*

The Apostle Paul put it this way: ... "That which may be known of God is manifest in (or among) them; for God hath showed it unto them. For the *invisible things of Him* from the creation of the world are *clearly seen* being understood by the things that are made; *even His eternal power and Godhead;* so that they are without excuse." (Romans 1 19 thru 20).

So then, we humans *are capable of perceiving* that there is an *unseen reality*; an essence below the material surface of all things. By this we know then, that all visible; or sensibly perceptible things have a natural purpose that is determined by a supernatural source. *In our reverential journey through God's mind, we recognize the fact that He intended from eternity, for His intelligent creatures to use the powers of reason, intellect, conscience, and intuition to "clearly see"; or perceive from all creation the evidence of his being.* This "seeing", or ability to perceive unseen reality is the faculty of "faith" that God bestowed upon man to inspire him to praise and worship his Creator, and to enable him to entrust the gift of life he possesses to the care of Him who gave it.

This faith is a natural attribute; or capability supernaturally bestowed upon all human beings. It is a fact that "*believing*" is part of the human makeup. *Believing* is germane to our ability to live and function in the world. All of man's achievements follow a process of conceiving and believing before finally achieving. People *believe* in many things and formulate their sense of reality based on these beliefs; this is faith.

But it is only man's *faith in God* that pleases Him.

This faith can only be expressed by means of communion between God's Spirit and man's spirit; for it is only man's spirit that allows him access to the higher dimension of reality where God abides.

But herein lay man's awful dilemma: He still possesses his God-given faculty of faith that he may fully exercise in the *natural* things of this sense-ruled material world. But the *spiritual* aspect of his nature has become fatally impaired.

God's man has been corrupted through his disobedience. Sin has activated death in him.

So, death started its work from the highest aspect of man's nature; indeed, that part of man through which God would lead and guide him; his spirit.

Death would continue, going on to invade man's *soul* and *body* culminating its work that began at *the end of man's life signaled by the departure of his spirit.*

Man, in his spiritually and morally fallen state, is still able to believe in the existence of God, but his corrupted and distorted human faculties can no longer "clearly see;" or perceive the invisible things of God.

And then, there are many things people *can* believe, but *will not.* This is because belief also involves *desire* and *choice.*

All men can believe in God, but many do not choose to, for in them is no desire for Him. They love pleasure rather than, or instead of God. Hedonism is also idolatry.

Man may still be able to say from an earth-bound, sense-ruled belief that "there is a God;" but in his fallen state, *he can no longer proclaim with transcendent faith born out of spiritual communion, that God is!*

It is a sure word that "he that comes to God must believe that He is…" It is also a sure word that "none can come to Jesus the Son of God except God the Father "draws" him." Again, it is a sure word that "As many as received Him, to them He gave the power; or legal right to become the children of God.

While it is true that He made us rational creatures, God has called His children to prove to a watching world, the infinite superiority of an enduring faith in divine inspiration and revelation.

In fact, the noblest thing that human reason can do is subordinate itself to the higher reality of spiritual revelation seen through the eyes of faith; for you see, *the essential nature of all things is spiritual.* Human reason however, cannot subordinate itself to a "dead"; or inoperative spirit that is no longer capable of "receiving the things of the Spirit of God." (1st Corinthians 2 14)

Because this is true, lost humanity must wander to and fro within the realm of moral and spiritual darkness trusting in defective human faculties to guide them. But man was not created by God to "direct his own steps." He was not designed to live and function in the world independently of his Creator. The fact is, no creature anywhere, on any plane of existence, was so designed. Absolute independence is a divine quality of life enjoyed by God alone. In fact, it is rebellion, or the spirit of independence that is the root cause of all evil in the universe. We shall discuss more on this at a later point in time.

But in review, let us keep the following points in mind:

- Humans *are capable of perceiving* that there is an *unseen reality.*
- This "seeing", or ability to perceive unseen reality is the faculty of "faith."
- *This faith is a natural attribute; or capability supernaturally bestowed upon all human beings.*
- *Believing* is germane to our ability to live and function in the world, but *it is only faith in God that pleases Him.*
- Genuine faith in God can only be expressed by means of communion between God's Spirit and man's spirit.
- Through disobedience, the spiritual aspect of man's nature has become fatally impaired.
- Man may, by his sense-ruled, earth-bound "faith" still believe "there is a God" but in his fallen state, *he can no longer proclaim with transcendent faith born out of spiritual communion, that God is.*

CHAPTER 10

His Will and His Ways

Nothing will so thoroughly convince us that in truth, we know nothing, like the study of God.

Nothing can so deflate the ego; nothing can so interject real humility into the mind like just a glimpse into the exceeding greatness of the wisdom of God.

There have always been naysayers declaring that there exists no tree of the knowledge of God while His believing, seeking, children enjoy the fruit of it.

It is a great tragedy that countless multitudes have lived and died without ever knowing their true purpose for having been born into the world. Having all their hopes and dreams confined to the visible world of the senses, many of them lived out all their natural lives "dead" to spiritual reality. And while many acknowledged the fact that "God is", they had no desire to pursue Him, for their hearts treasured this sin-infested, perishing world.

It is a fact that it is impossible to safely arrive at a right understanding of God's eternal purposes without an understanding of what is revealed about His nature and character. And we must understand that God does not reveal His ways to those who have no desire to know Him unless it is for the merciful purpose of kindling that desire in them.

For those of us who desire to know His will, His ways, and that which he would reveal of His eternal plan, we are encouraged. For it is He who first pursued us instilling in us a desire to pursue Him. And He has promised in His word that "He is a Rewarder of them that diligently seek Him".

We, as humans, can observe the actions of other humans and make some sense out of those actions based on some understanding of our own human makeup. But how are we lowly lumps of animated clay supposed to examine the divine nature? Such a suggestion sounds absurd!

Indeed, it <u>is...</u> absurd. Shall the clay examine the Potter?

Yet we go forth undaunted by the self-consciousness of our human frailty because we have faith that the path we have taken is according to the will of God. It is not presumption; it is faith in God. Genuine faith in God pleases Him. In fact, without it, pleasing God is impossible!

So then, let's just begin right there.

<u>Divine pleasure</u>….

It is the simple, yet profound reason behind all creation!

Everything that God has wrought has been because it has pleased Him to do so.

He has been under neither constraint, nor obligation at any time to any creature.

He has never known lack, nor experienced the discomfort of compelling need.

God simply does what He wills to do.

Nothing in all of creation can restrain His movement, nor presume to bring correction or rebuke to any of His actions.

Yet, while it is true that God's will is completely free, it does not follow that His will is expressed or exercised without limitation. He can do anything He wills to do, but He cannot do what He does not will to do.

In other words, ***God <u>can</u> do anything He chooses, but He <u>will not</u> do anything He has not chosen to do.***

Let us move a little slower on this point.

Now consider and recognize the fact that ***"freedom" is <u>not</u> the opposite of "limitation".***

For example: one may dine at a restaurant that offers a smorgasbord menu. The sign will probably read something like this: "All you can eat for only 12 dollars."

In this case, the patron may eat freely as much as he desires. No one will forbid the size or number of portions of food on the menu that the patron enjoys. But there are *internal limitations* within the patron.

If his stomach can only hold one plate of food, he cannot consume six plates; nor can such a desire be found in him.

He is free, but he is not without limits. He must enjoy his freedom within certain divinely-set parameters of his physical human makeup.

It is impossible for him to sustain a *desire* for more food after his stomach is filled to maximum capacity if his intellectual and emotional faculties are intact.

The fact is, without limitation, there cannot be order. Wherever all limitation and restraints are removed, there is anarchy and chaos.

An unrestrained person is out of control and dangerous.

Can we see then, that <u>while there are no limits to God's power, there are certainly limits in the way He uses it.</u>

God never does what He does simply because He can.

<u>God's actions are not power-based; they are character-based.</u>

This is where "limitation" comes into play when we speak of God doing whatever He wills.

You see, His will is born out of His desires; and all His desires are born out of His nature and character.

<u>His nature is love, and His character is holy</u>.

If we seek to rightly understand what God has revealed of His eternal plan, it is necessary that we understand fundamental truths regarding His nature and character.

These things are the foundation upon which bible doctrines must rest.

So then, at the outset, let us establish the following fundamental truths:

(1) <u>God; our Creator, desires for us to know Him</u>; in fact, it is essential that we do. He has spoken to men, inspiring them to write down what He has shown them.

<u>The Holy Bible is the inspired record He has left for us.</u>

(2) <u>He is Sovereign Ruler over all</u>. He has never relinquished His authority, nor ever been subject to any authority but His very own. He has never sought to regain control over anything at any time because it is impossible for Him to lose it.

(3) <u>God will never act in a manner contrary to His eternal, unchanging nature and character</u>. The omniscient, omnipotent, omnipresent eternal God performs every action according to the flawless perfection of His being.

(4) <u>Life was designed to be lived in the light of God's eternal truth.</u> Man's inbred religious nature was meant to find its fulfillment and highest satisfaction in the worship and service of the only true and living God who is revealed in the Holy Bible.

(5) It is a wonderful truth that God, our creator, desires for us to know Him.

(6) It <u>is also, a reasonable truth considered in the inspirational light of the Holy Scriptures</u>;

for God fashioned man "in His own image and after His own likeness."

He has extended to us, an invitation to come unto Him and to know Him intimately.

(7) <u>Even still, no creature will ever "plumb the depths" of the knowledge of His being.</u>

"How unsearchable are His judgments and His ways past finding out."

There is no taking the mystery out of God. He can only be known in the ways He has chosen to reveal Himself. Yet what can be known of God is so vast and full of wonder that the entire host of witnesses from the beginning of time to the present cannot tell it all!

As the Author of Life reveals more and more of Himself, the diligent seeker begins to find greater and greater meaning and purpose in the world around him.

Existence is transformed into adventure.

We begin to see that it is through our right understanding of God that we come to rightly understand ourselves.

The opposite is true as well. It is through our misunderstanding; or ignorance of God that we come to misunderstand ourselves. And at best, we can never even fully determine what we ourselves are; for our true identity is hidden within the mystery of the divine purpose of God.

God is; and because He has so determined; we are.

Only <u>He</u> is infinitely wise. Only <u>He</u> truly knows. Only <u>He</u> is omnipotent. Only <u>He</u> is self-sufficient and self-sustaining. And while true that we are made "in His image and after His own likeness," we must never fail to make the distinction between ourselves and our maker.

Origins may never be attached to His person; He is ever the Originator.

Let us determine at the outset that ownership of all things belongs to God. Man; the creature, owns nothing. The angels of Heaven own nothing. The Devil and the hordes of hell own nothing. Yahweh God is LORD of all.

Let us further determine that we know nothing; and can of ourselves, accomplish nothing. True knowledge is absolute, and pure power is unlimited, belonging singularly to the only-wise God.

I believe that our pursuit of the knowledge of God must be preceded by a clear and humble recognition of His infinite superiority and uniqueness. Let us take time to be still and tremble in reverential fear as we consider His awesome holiness. For this is where the divine impartation of wisdom begins.

The principal aim of our subject: "Life" A Journey thru the Mind of God"; is to inspire in us faith in the infinite goodness and wisdom of our God, and to celebrate the wonderful future ahead for all who trust in Him.

We cannot explore all that is contained in the infinite mind, but we can know those things He is pleased to share with those of us who yearn to know Him.

His word is infallible; His purpose, immutable, and His ability to accomplish all His pleasure, unlimited.

In one sense, He is indeed an impersonal force. He is in fact, the "source" of force.

He is the God over all forces. The Scriptures inform us that: "There is no power (or authority) but of God; and the powers (authorities) that be, are ordained of God." (Romans 13 1)

Whether the forces be natural or supernatural; elemental or intelligent, they have their origin and empowerment from God.

On the other hand, if by "personhood" we mean that which is characterized by absolute uniqueness and exclusivity, then He is *the only true existing Person.*

For God cannot be merely a "person" among other persons without being identified as one of a *'kind."*

But He is not a "kind" of anything; He just is! He is not three persons; He is one God.

For whatever "personhood" is defined as, "Godhood" is higher. If we insist on describing Him as a person, then He in fact, is the only *true* person.

Angels and men should then, only be assigned to personhood in a secondary sense.

Considering God's reality, we are merely "sub-persons."

The personification of God is a human necessity, not a divine one.

If *"genuine"* personhood could be ascribed to us, it would include <u>all</u> of us collectively, for it is only in <u>that</u> sense that we are unique or exclusive.

But I suggest that rather than talk about God as one "Person" or three "Persons", we should stay with God's revelation of Himself found in the Holy Scriptures. **"I, the Lord, am one God,"** says He.

"I Am that I AM," says The Almighty.

God is one, and He "will be what He will be."

Everything else "is" because God has decreed it to be so.

Now as we must understand that God does what He wills, or according to that which pleases Him, we must <u>also</u> understand that *there is a central object of His pleasure and affection.*

Now listen very closely to what I am about to say and give it deep consideration.

<u>**It is God's love nature that moved Him to prepare for Himself a body.**</u> **(Hebrews 10:5)**

The Word of God, who is truly God in all His fullness, came forth out of the omnipresent Spirit to "personify" God to the creation that would follow His coming forth.

Yes, God "took on" what we would call "personhood" for the sake of all that his own hands would, thereafter, create that they might have fellowship with Him.

In the course of time, we would come to know Him as His only begotten Son Who in fact, as the Word, is how all creation came into being. (John 1 3; 1 14)

Before any creative act of God, He prepared for Himself a bodily presence. (Hebrews 10 5)

The Word would be made flesh and dwell among men.

In loving His Son, God was loving Himself, for He who is the Word, whom we came to know as the Son, was with God (as the express image; or "Person" of Him.), and was indeed, very God.

Of course, God loves Himself. All that He wills to do is for His own pleasure.

It is foolish and shallow thinking for any of us to deny this.

All things were made by the Word made flesh known to us as the Son.

All things were created *by Him* and *for Him*. (Colossians 1 16)

To find this truth offensive is to reveal sadly, how humanly many portray Him in their thoughts.

If He who is excellent in every way; the source of all beauty and wonder, did not love Himself, are we to accept that He hates Himself; or harbors some regard for Himself somewhere between these two extremes?

It is His love nature including love for Himself that moves Him to bestow love on the works of His own hands.

Before there was anything, He was there being love; and as surely as there was nothing else to love, His nature could only find expression in the love of His own infinitely glorious person. That is why all things were made by Him and for Him. They were made by Him because He is the Creator. They were made for Him because there was no one else for whom they could have been made. No one else existed!

The fact is, that one of the simplest, yet profound definition for love is "good will". Jesus taught us to love our neighbor as ourselves because he understood that loving others was first based on loving ourselves.

No one loves unconditionally; not even God. His love for believers is based upon His love for His Beloved Son "in whom He is well pleased." The love of God is "in" Christ Jesus, our Lord. The love of God is bestowed upon believers thru our "abiding" in Christ, who is the sole representation of that which fully pleases Him.

When we think of the love of God, we need not think of the common expressions of love displayed by natural men and women born out of their self-centered Adamic natures.

God's love is self-centered as it should be. For us to think otherwise is merely a failure to think deeply enough about the difference between God and His creatures.

This love flows outward from its center; or His innermost self unto all creation and returns to Him.

I deliberately use the words "creatures" to describe both the highest-ranking angels and the most noble of men. I do so to remind us of the exceeding greatness of God.

He must never be evaluated according to human standards.

Men may be proud and arrogant, but it is impossible for God to be so.

How can God think too highly of Himself? Whatever "highest" means, it is He who defines it. God loves Himself because the very nature of love requires Him to do so. The only thing that can stimulate His desire is the beauty of His very own pristine holiness.

Almighty God loves Himself because that which pleases Him; those qualities capable of kindling His desire can only be found within Himself. It is the reason He sent forth out from Himself into the world the very expression of His being whom He identified to us thru the Apostle John as the Word of God.

John continues to unfold the revelation of Emanuel "God with us" explaining that the "Word was made flesh and dwelt among us." God had miraculously made His way into the world and would be recognized by those who believed on Him as the Son of God.

Finally, there was in the world among men, one to whom the love of God could be drawn without reservation; one who fully pleased God. John shares with us that the Word made flesh was Himself, very God. So then was God loving God? Of course, He was. And his love for us is possible only in our abiding in the perfection of his Son.

That is the reason why God, who, in the process of time became a divine biological Father, said to His Son, "Thy throne oh God is forever" (Hebrews 1 5 thru 8) Prior to this time, God had never been a divine biological Father. Prior to this, there was no only-begotten Son of God. Those who recognize The Lord Jesus Christ as the "eternal" Son of God are mistaken if by this designation, they mean to say He was always the Son from eternity. Read Hebrews 1 5 again. God says: "You are my Son. Today I have become your Father." God was speaking from eternity making a declaration clearly associated to the realm of time.

If we will detach ourselves from thinking of God according to human standards, we will understand that He should not be explained as a "trinity." May I reverently say to you in the presence of God, that He remains "One Person" while functioning as the Father, Son, and Holy Spirit. The multiple operations of God are the operations of Spirit. God is Spirit; not (a) Spirit as has been erroneously expressed in some translations. We must understand that to see Him as "a spirit "is to identify Him in a class with others. God is not an anything that we can conceive; He is altogether

"Other." We cannot make Him one person or three persons according to the conventional use of the term just because it makes describing Him more comfortable for us.

There are three distinct descriptive things said about God in the Holy Scriptures:

<u>God is love</u> (1st John 4:8); <u>God is spirit</u> (John 4 24) God <u>is light</u> (1st John 1 5)

These three things are principal identifying characteristics of the unfathomable reality we call God.

If God is love, then wherever love is present, God is present.

God is Spirit; or that which produces life (John 6 64) Many manifestations of life are temporary, but life itself is a product of spirit. As a matter of fact, the terms "spirit" and "life" are practically synonymous. Spirit simply becomes life when it infuses anything. So, then life is spirit imparted. Nothing lives unless life, of course indwells it; in fact, it is not life unless it indwells something.

Here is a revelation concerning this matter of life. <u>All life is eternal</u>... This means that the phenomenon called life will always exist. It does not mean that every living thing has eternal life; but that the life within it is eternal, even if that thing at some point must be separated from life.

It means that the mystery called "life" will survive for all eternity, for spirit will never stop producing life. And why are we assured of this? It is because love requires it. Love places a demand on spirit to produce life.

Spiritual light is manifested truth or…truth made visible; or pure intelligence; rightness; and goodness abiding in a recognizable context.

Certainly, truth must have an abode. Wherever eternal truth abides is holy. Eternal truth must be represented by that which it represents. Eternal truth represents God and can only be represented by Jesus, who said He was the (eternal) truth. The truth (about God) was in Him and represented Him by His every word and deed; and He represented the truth by the same means.

In the order of God's creation, the heavens and their innumerable hosts came first; the earth was created afterwards. (Genesis 1 1) Among the host of heaven within the angelic realm, there occurred an insurgency; a rebellion. Prior to this uprising, there had been universal peace and joy, for every spirit was in submission to the will of the Supreme Spirit; God Himself. But now, even as you read the words of this writing, the ramifications of that ancient rebellion are being felt and witnessed among the entire population of planet earth.

To be sure, the mighty army of the Lord of Hosts is alive and well! Heaven is secure, and the Lord God Omnipotent reigns! Glory to His Great Name Forever! It is impossible for us to number the existing multitude of holy angels and heavenly beings that God called "stars" and "sons". In one place, the angels are called "an innumerable company". (Hebrews 12 12)

Yet there remains a "renegade company"; an evil network of cursed spirits whose aim is to wreak havoc among the children of men. Human history begins with seduction, deception, spiritual indifference, guilt, fear, denial, alibis, accusations, self-willed worship, violence, death, curses, banishments, alienations *all within the first family!* A continuum of these same things and more has been consistently experienced in our world from then until now; and tomorrow's forecast assures us that there is yet more to come!

Nevertheless, despite the bleak and miserable picture displaying itself across the canvas of the faithless world of fallen humanity, there is another glorious portrait! In it, we may behold the emergence of a magnificent spectacle upon which bright heavenly light shines. A mighty voice speaks from heaven concerning it: "The gates of hell shall not prevail against it!" Then we, who are called by His name, remember. Yes, we indeed remember the glorious Light that came down from heaven and shined among men. Our hearts begin to swell with waves of thanksgiving and praise as we remember. Our faith is enlarged as we recollect the promises and rest in the assurance that despite the ongoing warfare, our ultimate victory has already been won. "Be of good cheer; I have overcome the world", Jesus said.

May we come to see ever more clearly, the revelation of God's glorious eternal purpose for His creation as it is revealed in His holy word.

The word of God is replete with inspired passages that expose divine purpose to us. By the grace and mercy of God, may the eyes of our understanding be enlightened.

Young Elihu reminded Job and his three friends of a powerful truth. He said: "There is a spirit in man, and the inspiration of the Almighty giveth him understanding."

Let's pray. Father God, we thank you for spiritual understanding as we consider the revelation of your will and eternal purpose in Christ Jesus, our Lord. May the Spirit of Truth preside over us shedding spiritual light in Jesus name: Amen.

As I said before, God simply cannot be classified. If He is, in fact, a person, we must first remove the "a" and then, utter the sentence correctly, stating that <u>God is Person.</u> In this case, all other intelligent life must be identified by some other classification, for "personhood" has been reserved for God.

So, let us now look back and summarize what has been discussed in this chapter thus far, and identify the key points:

- Understanding that which God's word reveals about His own nature will help us in our understanding of His eternal purpose.
- All that God has created and purposed to do in Jesus is ultimately for His own pleasure.
- Although God is omnipotent, His choices and actions are not power-based; they are character-based.

- The entire universe is structured on the principle of *relationships* and God wants all people to know Him.
- For man, growing knowledge of God translates into increasing understanding of himself and his true purpose.
- Jesus Christ is the object of God's love and God's eternal purpose is centered in Him. Divine favor is bestowed upon them who "abide" in the Son of God.

CHAPTER 11

The Searcher of hearts

<u>Man's capacity to believe may always be translated into trust.</u> But we must see that believing and trusting, though inseparable, are not synonymous principles. To believe is to *accept* a thing to be true. To trust is to *depend upon* a thing to be true.

Many people declare that they believe in God. I am sure that this declaration is true. However, to many, this idea of "believing" goes no further than a vague mental assent; a detached acceptance of a concept.

A person may have been brought up in a home in which it was commonly accepted that "there is a God." Such a person may also accept that this idea is true. Yet throughout all the years of his life, he may never consciously *depend* upon this information. To him, God may be accepted, but not considered relevant so far as life applications are concerned. In school, I was taught that the earth is 93 million miles away from the sun. I believe that this piece of information is true. Yet in all the sixty-six years of my life, I have never *depended* upon this information. When I was taught it, I accepted it to be true, so I believed it.

But I tell you, if I were suddenly informed by the scientific community that the earth was not really 93 million miles from the sun, but rather, 94 million miles away, I would not be troubled. Why? Because I never *depended* upon that information. It was never important because for me, there was in it, no life application.

And so, it is, for many regarding their belief in God. It is a sort of "believing that actually doesn't matter much to them. But what they don't realize is the all-encompassing significance of God's existence. Nor do they perceive that such a quality of belief that advances no further is in the sight of God, the equivalent of unbelief. It is faith without corresponding action; or as the Bible calls it; "dead" faith (James 2 17). God looks at these empty confessions and sees no life application. Dead faith will do for languishing souls about as much as empty bowls will do for the hungry.

But what must be understood here is that this condition of *dead faith* is not simply the experience of a few, or even many foolish individuals, but is in fact, an experience shared by every single descendant of Adam. For you see, when the scriptures speak of dead faith or even no faith, they are not meant to indicate that the faculty of faith; the capacity to believe and trust is non-existent. But *dead faith* speaks of the <u>absence</u> of a specific *quality* and *focus* of this universal human capacity. In other words; *something is missing,* and that missing thing is the reason for its *distorted focus* and *misdirection regarding its most vital purpose.* Man was created to live in eternal fellowship with God. So then, faith that looks to, and relies upon the true and living God is clearly focused and rightly directed.

But dead faith is the inheritance of all the descendants of Adam.

Believing is primarily, a matter of acceptance; *trusting*: primarily, a matter of dependence. To believe is to *accept* a thing to be truly as you conceive it to be. To trust is to, in some way, *depend* upon the thing believed. And it is easy to see then, that those who truly believe in God also naturally trust Him.

Therefore "believing" in the *biblical sense* of the word involves *more* than mere mental assent, and that is why in scripture, the use of the term is accompanied by some action. When a person truly believes in God, his actions will correspond to that belief in such a way that trust is thereby demonstrated.

But let's take a closer look at this "trust" thing because it is a matter of utmost importance. For with our mouths, it is easy to make great confessions of faith that are inconsistent with the true state of our hearts. But faith that moves mountains is not the result of an empty monologue. There are enemies within us that stand in opposition to the establishment of our trust in God. Enemies like doubt and fear leave many "frozen" in a state of immobility and indecision. Others are repelled by the hand of God himself as they proudly presume to move into the place of blessing in their own strength, ability; or righteousness.

On the other hand, those who see the power of God operating regularly in their lives have entered; and are abiding in that place of genuine trust in God. This is the fellowship God has always desired us to have with Him.

There will always be internal challenges to your faith, but the good news is that God has given us a mighty weapon to wage war against all these enemies within. It is the sword of the Spirit; the word of God.

The Apostle James informs us that a double-minded man is unstable in all his ways. There are some things that must be settled in our hearts during our lives before we expire. The primary thing is a wholehearted recognition of, and accountability to, the fact that God is!

God, who searches the hearts of men, examining the true nature of their innermost thoughts; seeks to find in them, a genuine awareness of their need for Him. For you see, if a man merely accepts the fact, or concept of His reality; such acceptance is insufficient to the Most High, for there can be no relationship established on such a foundation.

Yet with this being true, it remains that for a person to simply "believe in God" is at least, intelligent. His rudimentary belief may be far from acceptable to God as a final position, but at least such a man is not deemed thereby, as a fool. (Psalms 53 1)

The Receptive Heart versus the Unreceptive Heart

There is one thing however, that universally prohibits a person from coming to God: it is an unreceptive heart. *An unreceptive heart is a mind that <u>will not</u> believe.* Indeed, to be capable of believing that God exists is universally inherent in our human natures; but man has fallen from his original standing.

The problem with man in his fallen state is that he is a spiritually-dependent creature operating under the rule of a rebel spirit. Adam and his descendants have become the children of disobedience. (Ephesians 2:2) As it has been previously stated, m*an in his present condition, may believe that there is a God; but it is not the same thing as believing that "God is."* In the former case, one only needs to consider the subject, with or without any personal conviction, and conclude with the opinion that there is a God. Such belief is purely a matter of intellect.

This is different from the latter case that speaks of believing that God is. For to believe that God is, requires more than the flawed human faculties of imagination and reason. The belief that "God is" comes by *divine revelation* with *conviction of heart. Where there is no revelation and conviction of heart, there is no genuine belief that God is.*

Here is another important truth: *One may have a deep conviction of heart that God is, and still never seek Him.* Conviction does not automatically translate into submission. Evil spirits are deeply convinced of the reality of God to the point of trembling; yet they do not voluntarily submit their wills to Him. (James 2 19)

Certainly, man is capable of sensing and believing in the reality of a supreme being, but in his fallen state, such belief is merely *intellectual belief* and biblically, still classified as unbelief. Belief with conviction of heart *in God's revealed truth* not followed by repentance is biblically called *disobedience. Neither Intellectual belief* nor *disobedience* work to the saving of a person's soul.

Now let's examine the two a little more closely. To intellectually believe, may be as simple as to form a casual, unenthused opinion about there being "something out there." But let us not underestimate the power of intellectual belief. For there are those who are deeply convicted of the reality of a "god" of their own intellectual design, or imagination. In fact, some of the most heinous crimes in the history of mankind have been committed by those who have submitted themselves to those false gods.

For it is what we believe in our hearts (or minds) that guide our actions, thereby determining the state of our lives. While the lives of some are truly blessed, being covered with divine favor; the lives of others are tragically cursed with divine disfavor by way of rebellion and Satanic deception.

Biblically speaking, there are only two fundamental classes of people in the world: <u>believers</u> and <u>unbelievers</u>. According to the biblical definition, a "believer" is one to whom the true and living God has been revealed by way of a God-sent messenger. ("How then, shall they call on Him in whom they have not believed? And how shall they believe in Him of whom they have not heard? And how shall they hear without a preacher? And how shall they preach except they be sent?" Romans 10 14 &15)

All people who reject the gospel of Jesus Christ, regardless of whatever else they may believe, are biblically regarded as unbelievers.

This distinction is extremely important for us who are believers to see. Unbelievers may believe that "there is a God"; but believers, by faith in God's revelation, believe that God is! But spiritual understanding necessary to embrace even this initial truth comes by way of revelation.

So then, how can a natural man who is spiritually impaired (or spiritually "dead") receive a spiritual revelation?

The answer: God must speak to that "dead thing" in him. In so doing, <u>*the faith inherent in man*</u> *is awakened* to the reality of the true and living God. This faith does not begin with the intellect, but with the spirit of a man *quickened (or awakened) by God's Holy Spirit.*

This is not a <u>new</u> kind of faith; it is that same faith that he was born with. But now through the awakening of his "dead" or defective spirit, his faith may transcend beyond the realm of the natural. Nor does God arbitrarily and <u>automatically inject</u> "faith" into the hearts of some to the exclusion of others making some believers.

No; this is *to the receptive heart*, the *awakening of his spirit* to the reality of the true and living God. It is the shining of the divine light of truth upon the heart; the quickening of a "dead" conscience. It is God's invitation; His call. We must understand that *the gospel message itself is the power of God*; but not to everyone; only those who believe it. The saving power of God cannot be released in an unbelieving or unreceptive heart, for it is a person's faith that allows access. (Romans 1:16) It is impossible for a person to reject the gospel of Christ and still receive His saving grace.

When Jesus used the Greek word "helkuo" translated, "draw" in John 6:44, he spoke of the work of the Father inducing men to come to Him by means of the convicting power of the preached gospel. It is only when the seed of the word falls on good soil (a receptive heart) that the life-producing power of God is released. A man may seek after God and find Him, but only because God first sought after the man. But God will not awaken the spirits of people who reject the light of truth.

God will not draw to Himself those who will not believe the report of His messengers, for it is the words delivered by His messengers that He uses to draw them in the first place. Therefore, Isaiah asked the question in the 53rd chapter: "Who hath believed our report; and unto whom is the Arm of the Lord revealed?" If a man whom God has not drawn to Himself claims to know Him, the testimony of that man is false.

We must understand that the "drawing" of the Father is not an irresistible coercion leaving the will and desire of a person out of the matter. The drawing of God is His power working in those who receive the word. The apostle John said: "*But as many as received him*, to them gave he power to become the sons of God, even to them that believe on his name." "Which were born, not of blood, nor of the will of the flesh, nor of the will of man, but of God." (John 1:12 & 13) This passage makes it clear that receiving is synonymous with believing. But the invitation of God by means of the gospel may be *accepted* or *declined by man*.

Therefore, God also said through the writer of the book of Hebrews: "Wherefore (as the Holy Ghost saith, today if ye will hear his voice, Harden not your hearts…"

The prophet Isaiah asked the question: Who hath believed our report; and unto whom is the Arm of the Lord revealed?" (Isaiah 53 1) The answer to the second question in the verse is concealed within the first question. It is those who have believed their (the prophets) report to whom the Arm (or power) of the Lord would be revealed.

Indeed, "Faith *comes* by hearing" (Romans 10 17), but it is not *produced* by hearing.

In Romans 10, verse 18, Paul continues to develop the argument that the nation of Israel was without excuse in their rejection of Christ: "But I say, have they not heard? Yes, verily their sound (the preached gospel) went into all the earth, and their words unto the ends of the (known) world. Now look at verse 21. "But to Israel He saith: All day long I have stretched forth my hands unto a disobedient and gainsaying people."

These people "heard" but no faith was produced by what they heard. This is because no "new" faith is automatically produced by God in any man simply by his hearing of the truth.

The spiritually dead may hear, and the light of truth may shine in one's heart. The conscience may experience conviction of heart; yet for all this, that same person may harden his or her heart.

In such a case, faith did not come forth by the hearing of God's voice. The call of God is not an irresistible "dragging" by God of the selected sinner to salvation.

It is the supernatural influence of the Holy Spirit, speaking to; or "touching" the intuition, conscience, intellect, and will of a man to induce him to come to God.

It is called scripturally, the voice of God. It may be either obeyed or rejected by the will of a person. Therefore, God, in His mercy, warns us through His messenger: "Wherefore (as the Holy Ghost saith, Today, if ye will hear His voice, hardened not your hearts…" (Hebrews 3:7 & 8)

All men already have faith. Faith, as we said before, is an original human characteristic.

The faith the Apostle Paul is speaking of is God-inspired, but not God-produced, for God-produced faith was already in man from his original creation.

So then, it is the one and only faculty of faith inherent in all men that *comes forward* by "hearing."

It is called the faith <u>of</u> God because it is God-inspired (through the hearing of truth) and God-directed (through the obedience of man).

The writer of Hebrews (popularly believed to be Paul) said in 4 2: "For unto us was the gospel preached, as well as unto them; but the word preached did not profit them, not being mixed with faith in them that heard it."

In other words: "We heard it, received it, and placed our faith in it." "They also heard it, but they rejected it, thereby nullifying the saving power of God in themselves."

<u>God's Spirit searches the nature of all things' including the nature of God Himself.</u> (1st Corinthians 2 10)

The Spirit searches men's hearts revealing their secret motives to God's mind.

Then the Spirit; knowing the will of God, moves in, upon, and in behalf of that man accordingly. (Romans 8 27)

He reveals truth to, and bestows grace upon *receptive hearts* (John 7 17) (John 8:31 & 32)

He conceals truth and reveals His wrath against *unreceptive hearts*. (Genesis 6:5 thru 7) (Romans 1:18; 32)

Let us stop here and consider a few important definitions of biblical terms.

Foreknowledge: What God knows ahead of time; or before the time of it.

Predestination: God determining how things are going to turn out.

The Elect of God

Christ is God's Elect. (Isaiah 42:1) His Chosen One, (Matthew 12:18) and *all believers were foreknown* as a pre-determined class of humans *in Him* so that they, *in Him*, are God's elect; His chosen; *not as individuals, but as a <u>class</u> of humans.* (Ephesians 1:4)

Whether we speak of Israel; the Church, or divinely selected individuals such as the prophets, it is Jesus Christ that separates them unto God apart from all others.

About the Church, the "Elect or election of God is a pre-determined *category, or class of people* whose foreordained destiny is to be conformed to the image of the Son. (Romans 8:29)

These are not individually selected persons that God has predestined and irresistibly drawn into that class; it is the *class itself* that God has predestined. Those who make up that class have met the conditions of a right response to the gospel message.

The "apostate" are another class of men whose rejection of God have brought about God's rejection of them.

Perseverance is a *condition* of election, not a *consequence.* (John 8:31-32) Natural human beings will find themselves "drawn away" by many things that are not God. Something in their altered human nature finds no appeal in the God to whom a heretofore undamaged intuition would draw them. They are nature-bound; void of understanding or access to the things of God.

There is within them a "god instinct" but no God revelation. The life within them is "closed off" to the realm of the material. They have no ability to transcend these borders.

This is the present condition, but not the original condition of man.

But as surely as God is the Creator of man; so, man is the creator of gods. Indeed, man has constructed many gods according to his own preferences.

There is, however, only one true God. And the God who is, cannot be the mere product of any of a billion conflicting opinions.

It matters not how many imaginations, speculations, superstitions, or theories men may produce; only the God who is God, is God! And all that man could ever know of Him is that which He would choose to reveal.

Man may believe many things but only that which God reveals about Himself is true.

The Sovereignty of God is in operation in the lives of all men.

Here is an important truth. It is a divinely-set law of life: *God can never be mocked!*

Proud man may think to "dismiss" God from his thoughts, but man's supposed dismissal does not signal God's departure from his mind.

A spiritually-blind man does not understand that God holds every one of his thoughts in the palm of His divine hand. At any time, He can, and does turn a man's mind in any direction He chooses. (Proverbs 16 9; 21 1)

Ask Nebuchadnezzar (Daniel 4 30 thru 37); Ask Pharaoh (Exodus 7 13) Ask Howard Hughes!

The following is a principle of spiritual life. Please listen closely: God *causes* all men's *hearts* to direct them down certain divinely pre-determined paths.

For God establishes a man's "reality" according to what that man has chosen to accept as true. (Proverbs 16 9)

It is only when a man receives and embraces the revelation of God that he is walking in *true reality*.

Please understand the sovereignty of God.

He not only directs the paths of them who acknowledge Him in all their ways (Proverbs three 6) He also "releases" from His divine guidance, them who harden their hearts against Him into predetermined paths of destruction. (Romans One 28) God is not mocked!

Through my senses, my brain produces thoughts that my conscience either accepts or rejects producing certain feelings within me. I then choose to accept or reject what I think and feel. This becomes my belief.

At this point, *my own heart* will direct me down *the path God has prepared for me* according to what I have chosen to accept as true.

We must understand that it is God who designates the place to which all men arrive.

All of man's choices are confined within God's choices. There is no choice that man can make that does not serve God's purpose.

God simply allows a man to choose and then accordingly, causes his heart to direct him along a course destined to arrive at God's pre-determined place.

It is God who sees to it that "As he thinketh in his heart, so is he."

He also *causes* all men's hearts to produce the words that come from them. (Proverb 16 1 & 9)

This is what Jesus meant when he said in Luke 6 45, "A good man out of the good treasure of his heart brings forth that which is good; and an evil man out of the evil treasure of his heart brings forth that which is evil: *for of the abundance of the heart, his mouth speaketh.*"

Our hearts consist of what we think, feel, choose, believe, and produce.

Indeed, these are the elements of which our hearts are made.

Our thoughts stimulate our feelings and combine with them to influence our choices.

What we think, feel, and choose is what we believe.

What we believe; or accept as true is what our lives will produce.

If we believe falsehood to be true, it will produce deception in our lives.

If we believe the word of God to be true, it will produce correction in our lives.

God does not irresistibly "plant" into the minds of men all the thoughts and desires which fill their hearts; but He *does* "organize" their minds according to the desires produced by the thoughts they entertain. It is the spiritual principle of "sowing and reaping." (Galatians 6 7)

The essential truth of this principle is that *God is the "Designer of Every Consequence."* Let us understand that *according to God's sovereign will*, nothing may be "planted" into a man's heart except he first believes it.

This belief; or mental acceptance make the man's mind "fertile ground" for the "seed," or idea being planted, whether it be good or evil.

In other words, thoughts are actively or passively "planted" into men's minds according their own desires. This is what Solomon is saying in Proverbs 16 9: "A man's heart devises his way: but the Lord directs his steps." In other words: We can make plans, but the Lord directs our steps.

It is God's will to plant His truths into the minds of men so that through this means, He might prepare their hearts to direct them down the path of blessing.

If the mind of a man receives the truth of God, his spirit will be awakened. If not, the man will continue to walk in spiritual darkness.

Therefore, Jesus said in John 6 63: "the words that I speak unto you, they are spirit, and they are life."

It is the will also, of evil spirits, led by their utterly wicked lord and master, commonly known as "Satan," to plant evil thoughts into the minds, moving men to continue in their rebellion against their Creator.

Man himself, through the sinful lusts within, entertains thoughts and imaginations that gratify his spiritually-depraved carnal nature. James informs us of the process that leads man to temptation, sin, and death. In chapter 1, verses 14 & 15, he says: "But every man is tempted when he is drawn away of *his own lust, and enticed.*" "Then when lust hath conceived, it brings forth sin; and sin, when it is finished, brings forth death."

It is the divine law of sowing and reaping working inside the minds of all men processing their thoughts so that they produce the thing desired, good or bad. He gives us the fruit of that to which we have given our hearts. If what we have chosen is not God Himself, then it is a "god" of our own design.

There have always been men who *would believe* although they had not yet done so. Their hearts would receive, but had not yet been "touched" by the "Searcher of hearts." (First Chronicles 28 9)

The conscience of man enables him to, by acts of will, prepare the heart to receive the Lord; as John the Baptist put it, "Prepare ye the way of the Lord; make His paths straight." (Matthew 3 3) It is the "breaking up of the fallow; or hardened ground" of one's heart to which the prophets Jeremiah and Hosea referred. (Jeremiah 4 3; Hosea 10 12) God has raised up messengers like these throughout every generation because men cannot hear the call of God without a preacher; and how shall they preach except they be sent? God has never left himself without a witness (Acts 14:7).

No act of man's will, can make him acceptable in the sight of God, but the will may be exercised in a way to prepare one's heart for divine visitation.

Conversely, the will of a man may also be given over to evil things to such an extent that the restraining influences of divine mercy and human conscience may be removed. Such persons are described in the book of Jude as: "trees whose fruit wither; without fruit; twice dead and plucked up by the roots."

The preaching of the gospel is the universal declaration of the good news of salvation available to all men through the cross of Christ. It is the "good news" to "every creature." But it is only the call of God to the receptive heart. The unreceptive heart has disqualified itself.

God does not exercise His sovereign will to overpower the unreceptive heart and draw it to Himself. Not all men are called to salvation *though it is made available to all men.*

The Lord did not say that all men are called, but that *many* are called. (Matthew 22 14)

Listen to Paul's words in First Corinthians 1 26: "For ye see your calling, brethren, how that not many wise men after the flesh, not many mighty, not many noble, are called." This is because most of the "wise, mighty, and noble" after the flesh consider the preaching of the cross foolishness. (Verses 18 thru 23)

Any person who hears the gospel of salvation and comes to God based on it, is a part of that congregation known scripturally as "the *called* of God."

It is the receptive heart; that is, a heart that does not continually reject the voice of conscience; a willing spirit despite the weakness of the flesh. Even the hearts of men who appear by human judgment, to be totally corrupt, may be receptive hearts, for not everyone walking in darkness *loves the darkness* they are in.

Who will believe? Only God knows. "I the LORD search the heart, I try the reins, even to give every man according to his ways, and according to the fruit of his doings." (Jeremiah 17 10)

Who will come? Only those whom God will "draw"; or induce to come. Who will be "drawn"? Only those who are willing to be drawn. "…And let him that is athirst come. And whosoever will, let him take the water of life freely." (Revelation 22 17)

Upon whom then, did (and does) God "pour out of His Spirit? "And behold, I pour out of my Spirit? *All flesh!* (Acts 2 17)

This is the *enduement of power* that Jesus spoke of in Luke 24:49: "I send the promise of my Father upon you: but tarry ye in the city Jerusalem until ye be *endued with power from on high.*"

Does this mean then, that the prophet Joel, whom Peter quoted in the above passage, prophesied that God would "pour out of His Spirit" upon every single human being in the world? No.

The term, "all flesh" indicates that the nature of this divine outpouring was not determined by God based on race, gender, nationality, or any other such discrimination, but without respect of person.

The scriptures are clear that this divine outpouring was the carrying out of the promise of God, the Father. They are equally clear regarding to whom this promise was given. Acts 2 39 says: "For the promise is unto you, and to your children, and to all that are afar off, *even as many as the Lord our God shall call." We must not confuse the invitation with the outpouring.*

The call; invitation, or "drawing" of the Lord our God will be responded to by receptive hearts; that is, those who are willing to be drawn. These are they upon whom the promise of the Father will come.

God has made the same invitation to many who have refused to believe and will not obey.

Who are those that are identified scripturally as the "called" of God? those who receive and respond to the gospel.

The receptive heart regardless of the moral state of the person's life, is "fertile soil" for the "seed" of the word of God.

The unreceptive heart may produce a morally acceptable life according to human judgment, and still be "thorny ground" upon which the word of God will fall and prove unproductive.

It matters not that when one would do good, evil is always present with him. It is the attitude of heart, even in a man who desires to do good and fails, that the "Searcher of hearts" seeks to find.

It is the *"poor in spirit;"* or those who have come to recognize that they are spiritually impoverished who will have receptive hearts. For the attitude of the poor is one of dependency; as opposed to the attitude of the proud, which is that of independence. It is not about his moral performance; quite the opposite in fact. But it is about one's failed efforts to do good, leading to recognition of his utter need of the grace and mercy of God.

A famous wealthy person now deceased, was quoted as saying that "paying taxes was for the "little people." Many of the rich and powerful of this world see themselves independent, needing nothing, fully trusting in their riches. But a receptive heart may desire that which is good even while sin stirs within him evil desires. That is why fallen man is capable of, though inconsistently, sometimes doing good.

But his good is tainted by the mere fact that it *is his; good*. At the root of it is still, self-loving self-will; doing the good *he* chooses *his* way. Only those in whom the self-centered spirit of independence has been broken through the convicting power of the Holy Spirit; those who have come to recognize themselves as guilty sinners before a holy God; those who acknowledge their own utter helplessness with regard to making themselves right with God; those who have heard, believed, and joyfully received the good news of the saving grace of God through His Son, Jesus Christ; and have received Him as both Savior and Lord; those who continue in His word, thereby, becoming His "disciples indeed," may declare, with the utmost conviction of heart, through a living, spirit-filled relationship, that God is!

CHAPTER 12

You Must Be Born Again

Who Can See the Invisible?

Why is God invisible? If it is true as I have written, that God wants us to know Him, why then, is He invisible? *Did He really create us*; or did *we create Him?* (I speak as a fool here to arrive at a point.) Is it, as many of the atheists say; that "the idea of God" was born out of the ignorance of ancient man who could not explain the complex phenomena of the world around him?

Indeed, it is unquestionably true that human understanding of the material world has been gradual and progressive. But given the "quantum leap" from the earliest times in history to the present day, how much has man "closed the gap" on the quest to arrive at the question of the conclusive meaning of life? How close are we? If science has "really" brought us closer to this understanding; this "utopian awareness" where can the fruit of our progress be found?

What is witnessed hour by hour; day after day in America; this high-tech; scientifically; and "culturally advanced" leading world community is expanding violence; a rise in std's, increasing obesity, ravaging sickness and disease; social and racial conflicts; mental illness and depression on the rise, lies and deception at the highest levels of government; right-wing extremism and homegrown terrorism, religious scandals and apostasy; sexual insanity, and………..shall I go on???

It is an undeniable fact that man is "fearfully and wonderfully made". The capabilities of the collective human mind are astounding to say the least. Of all the creatures that occupy this planet, man alone, is endowed with the ability to *imagine*; or envision, believe, conceive, and ultimately *produce* the thing originally imagined.

Yet we must acknowledge the fact that of all the endowments of man to produce the thing imagined, only *one* of them (the body) is material; or physical; the rest are non-material; incorporeal, and yes……. invisible! If this is not so, then someone please tell us what is the color of our thoughts; and how much do each of them *weigh*? In what fragrance or flavor do they come?

Perhaps someone might produce a thought that I might touch with my hands.

Well the truth of the matter is that we *can <u>indeed</u> see, hear, taste, touch and smell thoughts*. Because there is nothing that man has produced in this world that did not originate with an *invisible* thought. <u>So then, the fact of whom; or what</u>

we truly are, is based more upon *unseen reality* than the transitory, fading, temporal nature of the material world we behold with our eyes. The point is; what we can see is perishing, while what we cannot see is eternal.

But then back to the question: If God is real and wants us to know Him, why is he invisible?

Now this may seem like a reasonable and intelligent question if simply taken at face value, but actually, it is neither very reasonable nor very intelligent. To address the question of God's invisibility, just consider for a moment:

How could an infinite, omnipresent Being ever possibly make Himself visible in all His fullness? How could He be the "visible" upholding of all things? How could we; (as the scriptures teach us) move and live and have our being in Him; in other words, be contained within Him while at the same time, see Him as an object to be observed from the outside?

In fact, if His full presence could be contained in a measure of space, He could no longer be deemed omnipresent. This would mean that something exists and extends beyond Him; outside of his creative jurisdiction, which would indicate that he is not truly Lord of all.

But here is the truth to be received by all of God's children: there is one God and Father of all, who is above all, and through all, and in us all. (Ephesians 4:6)

The fact is, when we speak of God, the word "beyond" must always come afterwards; and never before! It is right to say, "God beyond men" or "God beyond angels"; or "God beyond time"; or "God beyond the universe". We may properly say, "God" then, "beyond", but never: "beyond" then "God". For there is no such thing as a "beyond God" period!

Then again, if observing God in His fullness *were possible apart from looking upon the Lord Jesus, in whom all God's fulness dwelt,* what would be the effect of such? Would the great and proud analysts of the world go to work on the most monumental project of all time; analyzing God? I speak in humor to arrive at a more serious point.

Someone please help me here. Tell me, what appearance; what form could He take on that would fully represent His infinite nature and character? For instance, what form can "omnipresence" take on? And since having a bodily form lends itself to at least, a *general* estimation of one's strength, what should "omnipotence" look like?

No; the fact of God's *invisibility* is not the problem. It is our understanding of the phenomenon of *invisibility* that we perhaps, should take a closer look at. For it is when we come to the place that we rightly consider the reality of "the unseen", that the way of understanding will open to us in greater measure concerning many spiritual truths.

Truth and reality have always been hidden behind the symbolism of the visible. There is a kind of "seeing" that transcends the material world to which our basic senses respond.

It is when we recognize this that the phenomenon of "the visible" must "step down" from its ascended place of supremacy in our thinking, for it is a usurper.

The world view of so many of even God's people is so wrongly shaped because of carnal-mindedness; or materialistic thinking. (In this case, by "materialistic", I mean: corporeal; or limited to the realm of matter.) Indeed, it is because of this inflated view of the importance of the visible, that many cannot see the absolute necessity of faith. It is a faith-robbing perception of life and reality. **The truth of life and reality will <u>never</u> be revealed by the principles of human logic. All we can ever learn that way is more about the nature of the symbols**.

Unbeliever, the spiritual man in you must be awakened.

In St. John 3, when we consider the conversation of Jesus and Nicodemus, we immediately recognize that there is a communication barrier between them that has to do with the matter of invisibility; or unseen reality.

Nicodemus begins the conversation with a leading statement which is in fact, a veiled question: To paraphrase the statement, it would sound something like this: "Preacher, the general consensus is that you must be a man of God because you couldn't do the things you do unless God was with you." The "hidden" inquiry goes on to say: "We don't really know what to make of you because you don't at all, match our expectations of the Messiah". "Who in the world are you?"

Jesus, knowing the true nature of his statement, "cuts to the chase". "Except a man be born again, He cannot "*see*" (or perceive) the kingdom of God." Please notice that Jesus is not responding to Nicodemus after the fashion of the statement, but goes directly to the "heart of the *communication* problem. Jesus is saying in essence: "If you could perceive the kingdom of God, you would know who I am". Hearing the words of Jesus; with his natural hearing, that a man must be born again, Nicodemus, an educated man, reasoned within himself. The truth however, remained invisible to him. The most this honored Pharisee could think to do was offer what clearly seems to me, to be a shameless sarcasm in the form of a "stupid" question; "Can a man, when he is old, enter a second time into his mother's womb and be born?" It is impossible for me to see that question as even remotely sincere.

The problem was that this <u>religious man</u> *was not a <u>regenerated man</u>*. Spiritual reality was invisible to him.

The things we see with our natural eyes produce natural thoughts while eternal things remain invisible. All that we can naturally see will someday, no longer be. God has revealed to us in His holy scriptures that: "…the things which are seen are temporal; but the things which are not seen are eternal". - II Corinthians 4:18

Now if Nicodemus had been <u>able</u> to *understand* Jesus' response to his inquiry, the inquiry would have <u>never</u> been made in the first place.

In Matthew, chapter 16, Jesus asked his "born-again" disciples: (Note: They *were born again long before they were called Christians at Antioch if by "Christians", we mean "followers of Christ.)*"…but whom say <u>ye</u> that I am?" (verse 15) In the next verse, Peter answers: "Thou art the Christ; the son of the living God." Upon hearing Peter's response, Jesus immediately pronounces a blessing upon him and explains why. It is because Jesus knew that Peter was not speaking from *human speculation*, but had received *divine revelation directly from God*. If Peter had only human reason, or popular opinion to rely on, he would have fared no better than Nicodemus. Nor was his understanding a result of his, or the other disciple's proximate relationship to Jesus, thus giving them an advantage over others.

Jesus indicated that this understanding did *not come by natural means*. According to the report of the disciples, the best the crowd could come up with was that Jesus must somehow, be a re-incarnation of one of the long-dead prophets, or the recently martyred John the Baptist (verse 14).

Now I ask you; is it right to believe that Peter was already born again when he answered Jesus? If not, how is it that he, an uneducated fisherman, was able to see what the Scribes, Pharisees, and doctors of the law could not see?

Perhaps the reason is because it is possible for one to receive divine revelation <u>without</u> being born again. But then, if that's true, it would surely seem to clearly <u>contradict</u> a timeless and universal truth about the natural man that the Apostle Paul would later give in 1st Corinthians 2, for in verse 14, he says:

"But the natural man *receives not* the things of the Spirit of God, for they are foolishness unto him: *neither can he know them* because they are spiritually discerned."

So then, here, Paul informs us that <u>a man can neither accept, nor otherwise know spiritual things by the means of anything in his human nature</u>. *This is why unseen realities so easily trip us up.*

It is not that we children of God are merely "natural men." We have indeed, been "born again."

But the problem is, when we received the new nature, we did not shed the old nature.

Please listen closely here: Not every "Christian" has been born again, *but every child of God has*!

The Bible does <u>not</u> tell us that God's children first <u>called themselves Christians</u>, but that they were <u>called Christians</u> first in Antioch. - Acts 11 26 This title was given to them by the unbelieving residents of the city of Antioch.

The truth is, we cannot by this passage, tell specifically who it was that came up with the title and identified the children of God at Antioch by that name. But what <u>is</u> for certain in our world today is, that the word "Christian" is used to identify and represent things that do not follow the way of Christ at all. In this sin-dominated, perishing world, one can be a "Christian" and still not be a child of God.

Now look back at 1ˢᵗ Corinthians two at verse 12 where Paul would say: "Now we have received not the spirit of the world, but *the spirit which is of God* (Note: Not "the <u>Spirit</u> of God"(capitalized), but "the <u>spirit</u> <u>which</u> <u>is</u> <u>of</u> <u>God</u>.") *that we might know* the things that are freely given to us of God."

Did Peter have "<u>the</u> <u>spirit</u> <u>which</u> <u>is</u> <u>of</u> <u>God</u>" back then, <u>*before*</u> *the day of Pentecost; <u>before</u> anyone was <u>ever</u> recorded as having spoken with other tongues; <u>before</u> the crucifixion? Indeed, he did, for the spirit which of God is a reference to the Spirit of Christ. Not only did Peter receive it, but all the apostles, as well as 72 other disciples. And they received it before the day of Pentecost. Saint John 20:22 says that Jesus "breathed on them and said: "Receive ye the Holy Spirit". Jesus was imparting the Spirit back in old testament times as well. (read 1ˢᵗ Peter 1:11 & 2ⁿᵈ Peter 1:21) This is not the baptism of the Holy Spirit which they would shortly after experience; but the rebirth, or re-awakening of their own spirits through the direct impartation of the Spirit by Jesus. On the Day of Pentecost, those in the upper room; already born again, would then, be baptized, or filled with the Holy Spirit that had previously "awakened" their formerly "dead" spirits. This experience would be one of many subsequent "fillings "to come.*

If these things are so, then it certainly brings clarity to us regarding the matter of Peter's ability to receive revelation from the Spirit of God; it is because he had within him, "<u>the spirit</u> <u>which</u> <u>is</u> <u>of</u> <u>God</u>."

So then, <u>the Spirit of God</u> (God Himself) <u>could</u> <u>*reveal*</u> to Peter (by <u>the</u> <u>spirit</u> <u>which</u> <u>is</u> <u>of</u> <u>God; or the Spirit of Christ</u>)

that Jesus, his master, was in fact, the Messiah; or Christ; son of the living God.

Peter was able to *receive* this revelation because of the indwelling "spirit which is of God" which was within him "that he might know the things that are freely given" to us of God."

Again, Peter had not been filled with the Holy Ghost, which neither he, nor any of the Apostles received until the day of Pentecost; but he had experienced regeneration, or received *"the spirit of Christ"* which enabled him to know spiritual things he could not otherwise, know.

Ask yourself: How is it that any man or woman in the Old Testament could have enjoyed an intimate intuitive relationship with God without their sin-deadened spirits being regenerated?"

The baptism of the Holy Spirit was not given to *save* us, but to *empower* those of us who are *already saved*. The promise of the Holy Spirit was not given to unsaved men, but to all that would respond to the Lord's call to salvation.

No one receives the gift of the Holy Spirit before receiving the gift of salvation that comes to the repentant sinner. It is not that we, the children of God, are merely "natural men." We have indeed, been "born again."

And what is this experience of being born again?

- It is when the Spirit of God quickens, or gives life to our sin-deadened, flesh-dominated spirits through the living (rhema) word.
- It is the regeneration of the human spirit transforming it from *the spirit which is of the world*, to *the spirit which is of God*.
- It is a *spiritual awakening* that is a product of the "incorruptible seed"; the (rhema) word of God. – 1st Peter 1 23
- It is the *spiritual operation* of the (rhema) word of God *that produces saving faith in a receptive heart.* - Romans 10 16 & 17
- Consider the parable that Jesus taught about the Sower's seed, in the 4th chapter of Mark. Read the entire parable, and then focus your attention on verse 20. "And these are they which are sown on good ground; such as *hear* the word, and *receive* it, and *bring forth* fruit.... "Those represented in this verse are born again.

If becoming a child of God is synonymous with being born again, does this mean that at the point of our conversion, we were "born" into the family of God? No! The new birth is not what makes us children of God, but without it, we could never become the children of God. Those who live right intentionally and love fellow believers can be assured, according to 1st John 3:10, that they are the children of God.

God only has <u>one</u> Son by birth, --Jesus ("My <u>only</u> begotten Son," says God.)

We are <u>children of God</u> by adoption, but we are <u>children of light</u> thru the new birth.

In 1ˢᵗ Thessalonians 5:5 it says: "For you are all children of the light and of the day; we don't belong to darkness and night." Before our conversion, we were children of darkness, but thru the quickening of our "dead" spirits by the living word of God we have become the children of light; or as Jesus said; "the light of the world."

There were "lights" in the world long before the day of Pentecost.

Cain's godly brother, Able was a light and the first recorded prophet in history (for Jesus named him at the top of the list of slain prophets. Matthew 24:31 thru 35) Enoch was a light. Noah was a light; as was Abraham, Joseph, the prophets, and many others.

We must rightly understand that being "born again" is the awakening, by the Spirit of God, of our spiritual perception when our hearts embrace God's word. Our status as the children of God was afforded us by the <u>legal</u> process of adoption. That is why our Lord Jesus is not ashamed to call us brothers. (Please note that human gender has no relevance in that realm.)

Again; if the conversion; or new birth experience predates the Christian era, then how broad is the scope of this "born again" issue? How old is the concept, and unto whom does it apply? Is this a universal truth applicable to all men who have been quickened by the Holy Spirit throughout all generations? It is indeed.

Please consider whatever conclusion you arrive at in the light of the word of God and not according to your religious indoctrination.

I raise this point because in the world of mainstream organized Christianity today, it is a matter that is universally germane to the question of whether one is truly saved or not. Yet it seems quite paradoxical in that so many who claim to be born again seem to be "saddled" with the same difficulty of spiritual perception that Nicodemus was!

Being religious will never allow you to perceive the invisible. Simply being affiliated with a Christian fellowship will not do it. **A <u>surrendered</u>, <u>believing</u> <u>heart</u> must be visited and acted upon by the Holy Spirit.**

John the Baptist preached ***<u>repentance</u>** and **<u>preparation of the heart</u>*** in anticipation of the Lord's coming to receive Him. **As many as received Him, to them He gave the (legal) right to become the sons of God.**

Once we are born again (not a legal, but a spiritual process), we must continue in study and practice of the word of God (which is the "seed" of rebirth) and thereby, "walk in the light" of truth. It is through this process that living faith will open our eyes so that the problem of invisibility will be dispelled.

Who can see the invisible truth?

Those whose spirits the Spirit of God has regenerated; those who are born again; those who by faith in, and obedience to God's revelation have become the children of God. Any grace teaching that suggests or declares that how a believer lives doesn't matter because all sin or sins have already been forgiven is a lie. It is in fact, a damnable lie. If you practice a life of willful sin for which you never repent, you will perish. Your confession of faith and your church affiliation will count for nothing at the time of your accounting before God because the blood of Jesus does not cover a life of willful sinning. This is what Hebrews 10:26 & 27 NIV says: "If we deliberately keep on sinning after we have received the knowledge of the truth, no sacrifice for sin is left, but a fearful expectation of judgement and of raging fire that will consume the enemies of God."

Dear reader, if you are not saved and your heart has been convicted by the truths you have heard in this book, the time for repentance (a changing of your moral mind) and turning to Jesus is now.

- Simply acknowledge that you are a sinner alienated from God and totally incapable of saving yourself.
- Ask God to forgive you for all your sins through the only means He has provided for all humanity; that is; through the death of His Son. Ask Him to lead you to a faithful bible-believing & teaching fellowship of believers and trust Him to do so.
- By faith, confess with your mouth that Jesus Christ has become your Lord and Savior and give God

thanks because you have been born again and are now saved.

- You also have been adopted into the family of God and you shall receive the gift of the Holy Spirit.

Congratulations to all who received this invitation!

Praise God and welcome to the family of God.

Now let the glorious journey begin because:

"**Unto you it is given to know the mysteries of the kingdom of heaven.**" (Matthew 13:11;16)

It is a journey through the mind of God.

The End